Buried Treasures in the Classroom

Using Hidden Influences to Enhance Literacy Teaching and Learning

Amy Seely Flint
Indiana University, Bloomington

Mary Riordan-Karlsson
Karlsson Consulting

 **INTERNATIONAL** **Reading** **Association**

800 Barksdale Road, PO Box 8139
Newark, Delaware 19714-8139, USA
www.reading.org

The International Reading Association attempts, through its publications, to provide a forum for a wide spectrum of opinions on reading. This policy permits divergent viewpoints without implying the endorsement of the Association.

Director of Publications   Joan M. Irwin
Editorial Director, Books and Special Projects   Matthew W. Baker
Special Projects Editor   Tori Mello Bachman
Permissions Editor   Janet S. Parrack
Associate Editor   Jeanine K. McGann
Production Editor   Shannon Benner
Editorial Assistant   Tyanna Collins
Publications Manager   Beth Doughty
Production Department Manager   Iona Sauscermen
Art Director   Boni Nash
Supervisor, Electronic Publishing   Anette Schütz-Ruff
Senior Electronic Publishing Specialist   Cheryl J. Strum
Electronic Publishing Specialist   Lynn Harrison
Proofreader   Charlene Nichols

Project Editor   Tori Mello Bachman

Cover Photo. Jonathan A. Meyers

Library of Congress Cataloging-in-Publication Data
Flint, Amy Seely.
   Buried treasures in the classroom : using hidden influences to enhance literacy teaching and learning / Amy Seely Flint and Mary Riordan-Karlsson.
      p.   cm.—(Kids InSight series)
Includes bibliographical references and indexes.
   ISBN 0-87207-294-0
   1. Language arts (Elementary)—United States—Case studies.   2. Group reading—United States—Case studies.   3. Multicultural education—United States—Case studies.   4. Social interaction in children—United States—Case studies.
I. Riordan-Karlsson, Mary.   II. Title.   III. Series.
LB1576 .F48423   2001
372.6—dc21   2001000784

Dedication

We often associate buried treasures with pirate ships, explorers, and distant places, so we may not realize how many buried treasures we have in our very own classrooms. We also know that we need a treasure map to find the buried jewels, but unfortunately, when we enter our classrooms and begin making instructional decisions, we are not given treasure maps.

It is our hope that you think of this book as a treasure map as you plan your literacy curriculum. The stories, strategies, and resources offered will shed light on the complex process of meaning making and will help you to better understand the multitude of influences and interactions that can be found within each literacy event. In future discussions with colleagues, parents, or students, we hope you treasure your students' voices, actions, and interactions. So often they provide us with thoughts and ideas we never knew existed. We believe these hidden influences of meaning making can be discovered many times throughout the day. Each time you discover one, please celebrate its newfound richness.

The students and teachers whose stories we share in this book provided us with many insights and treasures that will stay with us for a long time. As we discovered the hidden influences of meaning making, we also discovered "treasured moments" in the classroom. We dedicate this book to the many students and teachers who have given us "treasured moments" over the years. We hope that you, too, will realize that you do not need a pirate ship to travel far distances to find the treasures—they are right where you are, in the classroom.

Contents

Note From the Series Editor

It is a pleasure to introduce readers to Amy Seely Flint, Mary Riordan-Karlsson, and the third- and fourth-grade students and their teachers presented in *Buried Treasures in the Classroom: Using Hidden Influences to Enhance Literacy Teaching and Learning*. In this book, Mary and Amy describe the literacy activities that occurred in two different classrooms—one in an urban community and another in a working-class suburb in the San Francisco Bay Area of California, USA. Throughout the book, we are provided the opportunity to look closely at how teachers and students create classroom learning communities, and how curriculum and routines define the processes by which teaching and learning occur. I am pleased that Amy and Mary's book has been selected by a respected panel of literacy experts to be published in the Kids InSight (KI) series; I believe their book makes an outstanding contribution to the field of elementary-level students' literacy development.

The KI series provides practical information for K–12 teachers and brings to the fore voices of and stories about children and adolescents as the basis for instructional decisions. Books in the series are designed to encourage educators to address the challenge of meeting the literacy needs of all students as individuals and learners in and out of our classrooms, while recognizing that there are no easy answers or quick fixes to achieving this goal. Sociocultural perspectives of how students learn are the foundation of each KI book, and authors address learners' emotional, affective, and cognitive development. Strategies and actions embraced by teachers described in KI books include

- dialoguing with other professionals,
- reading research findings in literacy and education,

- inquiring into teaching and learning processes,
- observing, talking with, and listening to students,
- documenting successful practices, and
- reflecting on literacy events using writing and analysis.

Authors of these books allow us to see into classrooms or view students' lives outside school to learn about the thoughts and dreams of young people, as well as the goals and planning processes of teachers. Finally, we are privy to how events actually unfold during formal and informal lessons—the successful and the less-than-successful moments—through the use of transcripts and interview comments woven throughout KI books.

In this book, the authors show us how to keep kids in sight by uncovering three key aspects of literacy lessons that are invisible to most of us as we examine teaching and learning processes. These hidden influences include stance—how teachers and readers perceive tasks and attend to texts during reading events, such as focusing on details in a story or finding links between a character's actions and our own experiences; social positioning—how children determine which peers to work with and how to interact during literacy events; and interpretive authority—how teachers and students judge the validity of others' responses during literacy events. Amy and Mary help us to see the complexities of these three influences by analyzing the tensions that arise when teachers and students have different purposes for literacy events, or when some children determine that they are able or unable to work with peers in fruitful ways.

Mary and Amy also help us glean insights as we examine the strategies teachers employ to address tensions that arise during literacy practices. For example, technology was a critical tool for learning in Lynn's classroom. Students used a video camera, the computer, and other tools to create and illustrate stories and poems. Work with and in the technology area of the classroom elicited a great deal of talk and negotiation between peers as they engaged in meaningful literacy activities.

In addition, the authors help us to understand what happens when teachers realize that their own perspectives about texts influence what they expect students' responses to be during discussions. Likewise, learners help us to understand how they position themselves during literacy events and how teachers' decisions about who works with whom affect a student's social position in the classroom and subsequently his or her literacy learning. For example, Kelly and Elizabeth's interactions while completing comprehension questions about the *Island of the Blue Dolphins* illustrate the concept of social positioning. We see that even though Elizabeth was smart and hardworking, she was not selected by peers for groupwork because she was positioned by her peers as undesirable: She had trouble working collaboratively on tasks and preferred to work alone, often ahead of others, on assignments. Kelly valued and expected to work together with Elizabeth, hoping the two could jointly construct responses for each question. Kelly and Elizabeth seemed to be well-matched partners from the teacher's perspective, but when we closely examine their discourse, we can see why their partnership did not work.

Throughout *Buried Treasures in the Classroom*, Mary and Amy help readers grapple with teaching and learning issues by urging us to write responses to questions posed, gather data from our classrooms, reflect upon what we see, and generate new possibilities for what could be. Mary and Amy help us to see that if teachers are willing to face the unknown and take reasonable risks in their pedagogy, we can move toward meeting the literacy needs of all students. The metaphor of buried treasure is most appropriate for the ideas in this book. Using the voices of and interactions between learners and teachers, Amy and Mary provide us with the tools to dig deeper—beyond the surface features of our literacy practices—to uncover gems of wisdom.

Deborah R. Dillon
Series Editor
Purdue University
West Lafayette, Indiana, USA

Kids InSight Review Board

Jan Turbill
University of Wollongong
Wollongong, New South Wales,
    Australia

Angela Ward
University of Saskatchewan
Saskatoon, Saskatchewan,
    Canada

Deborah A. Wooten
Glenwood Landing School
Glen Head, New York, USA

Josephine P. Young
Arizona State University
Tempe, Arizona, USA

Acknowledgments

There are many people we wish to thank for their support and encouragement in the writing of this book. First, we want to thank Lynn, Jane, and Kathy for inviting us into their classrooms and sharing precious time with their students.

Second, we extend thanks to Deborah Dillon, editor of the Kids InSight series, for encouraging us to share our story and for helping us weave our stories together over many breakfast meetings at IRA and NRC conferences. Our thanks also go to Joan Irwin, IRA Director of Publications, and to the International Reading Association Publications Committee, who have supported our efforts to keep kids in sight as we continue to view literacy through new lenses. Also, we thank Tori Bachman, IRA Special Projects Editor, for keeping us on track.

We thank our friends and colleagues—Paul Molinelli, Penny Dyer, and Marilyn Greco—who provided us with constructive feedback on earlier drafts of this manuscript. In our conversations we discovered many hidden influences in our own meaning-making process.

We also want to thank our families for their support and continued excitement throughout the writing of this book. Without their love and support, we would still be searching for our treasures. Amy wishes to thank her husband, Mike, and Mary thanks her husband, Sven, for their love and patience as we spent many hours on the phone and sending e-mails to craft our story. And appreciation goes to Mary's son, Lukas, who reminds us each day of the treasures we hold in our hearts and hands. May his quest for treasure continue as he grows, and may he never give up on finding the jewels.

We consider ourselves fortunate to have discovered so many buried treasures in our families, colleagues, teachers, and students. Each one has enlightened our thinking about and understanding of literacy.

The Hidden Influences Unveiled: The Story Unfolds

Lerissa, Sammy, Claudia, and Anneka sit at their desks and write in their The Courage of Sarah Noble *journals. They talk about the chapter they just read, titled "Indians!"*

"Sarah must have been scared of the Indians, but then she was really brave to play with the Indian children," comments Claudia. She continues, "I thought it was neat that they were able to play games even though they could not even talk to each other because they spoke different languages."

"I liked how she used hand signals to explain things to the Indian children," Anneka adds.

As the children write in their journals, they discuss their love of reading. Lerissa explains, "This was a good chapter. Now I want to read ahead and find out what happens."

"Yeah, me, too," adds Claudia.

Anneka responds, "Oh, Lerissa, you just love to read everything."

"Yeah, I do. I love to read because when I grow up, I want to be really smart, but not like nerd-smart, but smart."

Sammy chimes in, "I love to read because you can travel around the world without leaving your bed. I especially like it when it's raining out. You can stay in bed all day and just read. It would be cool if I lived somewhere where it snowed, then I could stay in bed on snow days and read…ahhh happiness!"

(The names of the children, teachers, and schools in this book are pseudonyms, although gender and ethnicity have been preserved.)

The central theme of *The Courage of Sarah Noble* (Dagliesh, 1991; all children's books are referenced in the Children's Book References on page 154) is about courage to face the unknown and willingness to take risks. The third-grade girls in the chapter-opening vignette share important insights about how bravery is an attribute to strive for, and how although the children in the story do not speak the same language, they are able to play together. As classroom teachers and teacher educators, we face similar challenges that in many ways remind us of Sarah's struggles in the story. We must meet the diverse needs of our students, whether in curriculum, language, or instructional practices. We therefore muster up our own courage, taking risks in our curriculum and instructional practices to discover what works for our students. We learn from our experiences, from each other, and most important, we learn from our students.

In a fourth-grade classroom, a group of children read and discuss The Mouse and the Motorcycle *(Cleary, 1965). This story, too, has elements of risk taking and courage, as Ralph, a mouse, and Keith, a young boy, become friends. At one point in the story, Ralph risks his life to locate an aspirin for Keith's illness. Throughout the book, the children enjoy the fictional narrative, while also investigating and wondering about some of the more realistic dilemmas that the characters face.*

The fourth graders begin a conversation about honesty and trust among children and adults. When Amy asks them to think about the dilemma Keith faces in trying to share his experience with classmates and teachers, Elizabeth reacts by saying, "I thought that he would because his friends might believe him." Robert adds, "Kids believe everybody." Kelly says, "I would if I was Keith's teacher, but I don't think grown-ups think a mouse can talk." Elizabeth then responds with, "Grown-ups don't believe kids all the time."

Following Elizabeth's comment, Kelly considers a possibility: "You could get a tape recorder, but then you wouldn't hear him." Elaine comments on this, saying, "Yeah, because he is so low." Robert adds, "If he yells, then maybe you could hear him." Marcy wonders if both characters could talk into the tape recorder.

The conversation between Elizabeth, Kelly, and Robert provides us with insights on what is possible when children have the opportunity to talk about their own concerns. Not only are the children addressing an important idea, but also their own interests have determined the direction of the conversation. The shared comments reflect a group of students who speculate about how adults do not always believe children and how they may be able to *prove* something exists. The children's comments seem to embody similar tensions that arise between teachers and students during traditionally structured literature discussions—that of teachers not quite believing students and directing the conversation to particular ends or outcomes.

So begins our story about the ways in which two groups of students, their teachers, and two university researchers (Amy and Mary) constructed understandings of texts, tasks, and each other. This book documents the successes and struggles as the teachers and students participated in a broad range of literacy-related events, from teacher-directed lessons to creative writing and collaborative discussions. Through the experiences of Lerrisa, Claudia, Elizabeth, Robert, and others, we examine those aspects of meaning construction that are often less visible and tangible, yet contribute greatly to how children and teachers respond to literature and interact with each other. New insights into these hidden influences on literacy development offer teachers and researchers opportunities to reflect on, and perhaps reconceptualize, current beliefs and practices, resulting in more informed instructional decisions.

Observing children's responses and actions contributes to our knowledge and understanding of the complex process of teaching and learning, in which we engage daily as educators and lifelong learners. Insightful teachers learn from their students. In the foundational book of the Kids InSight series, *Kids InSight: Reconsidering How to Meet the Literacy Needs of All Students*, Deborah Dillon (2000) describes insightful teachers as those who

> have the ability to see or perceive what counts during classroom lessons and interactions with students.… Insightful teachers have a sense of what is significant to focus on during an interaction or event; they have the ability to quickly sift out the unimportant features from critical ones. And they have the ability to understand the significance of what they see. (p. 16)

Insightful teachers then, not only listen to their students, but also are willing to take the instructional and curriculum risks required to push everyone, including themselves, to a higher level of understanding of texts, contexts, and each other.

Reflection Point 1.1 _____

Obtain a journal to record your reflections and wonderings as you read this book. In each chapter, we will ask you to reflect on your own beliefs, make connections to your own classroom, apply educational theories to practice, and share your ideas with your colleagues. In this first reflection point, jot down a few ideas about your own "insightful" teaching.

1. In what ways are you an insightful teacher?

2. Now share your ideas with a colleague. What practices does he or she list as insightful?

_____

What Are the Hidden Influences?

Teachers, students, curriculum, and routines create the context in which meaning construction is central to engagement and learning. These aspect of meaning making are quite visible to anyone observing in the classroom. Teachers and children interact to create a learning community, while the curriculum and routines establish the materials and processes by which learning and teaching occur. There are, however, less visible aspects that are hidden to the casual observer, including stance, social positioning, and interpretive authority (definitions of these terms are provided on the facing page, and they are further explained and expanded on in subsequent chapters). We believe awareness of these influences redefines what is meant by effective and meaningful literacy events. These hidden influences contribute to some of the underlying tensions that the three teachers with whom we worked faced within their classrooms. We also believe that having a repertoire of strategies to address these tensions may lead to responsive and insightful teaching.

Broadly defined, *stance* is the intention or orientation one has toward texts and tasks (Langer, 1995; Rosenblatt, 1978). When teachers and learners participate in literacy events, the underlying purposes are central to the resulting outcomes. There are many dimensions to stance, including ideological, contextual, and literary/strategic (see Flint, Lysaker, Riordan-Karlsson, & Molinelli, 1999, for a discussion on the dimensions of stance). For example, a literary/strategic stance considers what the reader attends to during the reading event, such as recalling information (for example, "How does Ralph get the aspirin for Keith?"), or connecting personal experience and character motivation (for instance, "Discuss a time when you felt similar to Sarah Noble, alone and afraid"). The ideological and contextual dimensions involve how teachers and students conceptualize literacy practices and how the classroom environment is established for literacy events.

Social position considers how peers perceive each other as members of the learning community and as viable partners for specific literacy events. From our observations of how children participate in various literacy events, we see that a child's social position is not permanent. Children construct their perceptions of each other based on academic performance, behavior, and friendship circles. The desire to participate or to invite another to participate is determined by a particular constellation of events. For example, in Lynn's class, Claudia often chose Lerissa as a partner, not only because they were friends, but also because she considered Lerissa to be helpful and encouraging.

Interpretive authority takes into account how teachers and students judge the viability and validity of responses shared within literacy events. This authority is dependent on a number of factors, including but not limited to social awareness, reading ability, and social positioning. To illustrate, when a reader in a literature discussion challenges or evaluates a peer's response, the reader is considered to have some level of interpretive authority. This authority often fluctuates depending on group composition. In Jane and Kathy's fourth-grade classroom, Kelly's competence in reading and knowledge of the teachers' expectations provided her with a sense of interpretive authority during teacher-led discussions. Robert, however, was less sure of the teachers' expectations, which resulted in him having less authority to share a possible interpretation. In other words, interpretive authority asks, "Whose responses are perceived as contributing to the meaning-making process?" In this book, we will explore these hidden influences through the voices and actions of children and their teachers in two different classrooms.

Introducing the Third- and Fourth-Grade Students

We (Amy and Mary) journeyed into two classrooms to share the stories and lives of a group of third and fourth graders in order to better understand the hidden influences that impact literacy learning in the middle elementary years. The classrooms in this study represent two distinctly different areas of the San Francisco Bay Area of California, USA—one urban community and one working-class suburb. There were eight focal children—students on whom we focused our attention—in the third grade and seven in the fourth-grade classroom. Descriptions of the focal children provide a backdrop for our discussion on the impact of hidden influences as the children participated in a variety of classroom literacy events.

Getting to Know the Third-Grade Readers

Lynn's third-grade classroom was in an urban elementary school located a few blocks from the campus of the University of California, Berkeley. Eli Elementary School comprised grades K–5, with approximately 322 culturally diverse students—52% African American, 33% Caucasian, 8% Hispanic, 5% Asian, less than 1% Asian Pacific and Pacific Islander—and Lynn's class of 23 children reflected this richly diverse population. Many of the children in Lynn's class had attended this school since kindergarten. Most were in the same multiage class (grades 1 and 2) for 2 years, so they were quite familiar with each other.

Early in the school year Mary explained to the children that she would be visiting the class to watch them read, write, play, and learn, and on occasion she might interview them. Based on their willingness to share their thoughts and ideas, and with permission from their parents, eight students (six girls and two boys) agreed to participate as focal students. The diversity in the students' reading abilities and in their levels of participation in various literacy events reflected the overall differences among all Lynn's students. As in all classrooms, these eight children brought a wealth of personal experiences and knowledge to their learning.

Brandi, an African American girl, was a fluent reader and a very independent thinker. She was quite confident in her reading and writing abilities and used her books as an escape. She loved to read and commented, "If I had all the time in the world, that [reading] is all I would want to do." Brandi often secretly read her Sustained Silent Reading (SSR) book when she completed math or social studies activities, or when the teacher was waiting for the class to settle down. Although somewhat social, she preferred to do many activities alone. Brandi's father was the physical education teacher at Eli Elementary, which delighted Brandi.

Jennifer, also an African American girl, was a struggling but enthusiastic reader and confided to Mary that she "likes nice stories, not sorta mean stories where they push each other around and they beat each other up." She was a talented artist who liked to write stories and draw wonderfully detailed illustrations. Jennifer was eager to learn new things, and she used her problem-solving skills whenever possible. She lived with her mother and was the youngest of five girls. Jennifer was new to this school, and at the beginning of the school year, she felt like an outsider. This feeling subsided over the course of the year.

Rodney, an African American boy, was a capable learner and quite confident in his abilities in all content areas, especially reading. He was "antsy" when required to sit in his seat for a long duration. Rodney worked quickly, aiming to complete his assignments first in the class. It was not clear if he did this to please his teacher or to move around as soon as possible. He was rather impatient when he was asked to redo any assignment or edit his stories. Rodney loved to read chapter books, especially ones that were somewhat scary, such as the Goosebumps series (Stine, 1995); he felt that the more blood and guts described in the story, the better. He also relished in writing these types of stories on the computer and adding graphics. At home, Rodney enjoyed reading to his younger brother and sister and visiting the library with his mother or grandmother. Rodney lived in a neighboring community and rode the bus to Eli Elementary each morning.

Tommy, also an African American boy, was a fluent reader who enjoyed reading mystery and adventure books with silly characters over and over again. Tommy exuded a great deal of confidence and had a vast amount of general and world knowledge, which he displayed in many forms. Although somewhat shy, he did raise his hand for nearly every question the teacher asked in all content areas. Tommy participated in the fifth-grade spelling bee, competing against his sister who was in the fifth grade. His mother, an active school community member, was in the audience, which gave Tommy and his sister more confidence in their spelling abilities. Tommy was a model student—diligent, polite, hardworking, and complimentary toward his classmates. He was intrigued by mathematics and had a marvelous sense of humor and adventure, which he put to use quite often in conversations as well as in his writing. When talking about his overall impression of the classroom, Tommy said, "The thing I like the most about my classroom is that it's not the meanest place you could ever be!"

The other four focal students described in the next section were the best of friends, and they loved doing everything together, including reading, writing, playing, and talking about good books and authors. Although they had very different personalities and read at different levels, they motivated each other to read and write creative stories. They had read most of the American Girl series together (e.g., *Samantha's Surprise: A Christmas Story* [Schur, 1986]; *Meet Kristen: An American Girl* [Shaw, 1986]; *Meet Molly: An American Girl* [Tripp, 1986]; *Meet Felicity: An American Girl* [Tripp, 1991]), and they were reading books from the Nancy Drew series (Keene, 1930) at the time of this study. Mary referred to them as the "literacy club," because these four students exhibited the many ways in which literacy was a part of their lives (see, for example, the opening vignette in which Sammy and Lerissa shared their reasons for why they loved to read). Oftentimes they acted out the stories during recess or class time. They thoroughly enjoyed the process of learning and giggled a lot along the way.

Claudia, a Caucasian girl, was a fluent reader who liked to read stories that taught her about plants and animals, or those that depicted friends and families in real-life situations. Sometimes shy in large groups, she was quite vocal in her intimate circle of friends. Claudia had a passion for animals as well as an artistic flare. She had contributed the class pet rat, Vanilla Bean, and shared responsibility for taking care of her. During her free time she loved to talk with her friends, play with Vanilla Bean, and draw illustrations of antique and modern fashions. She was extremely artistic and aspired to be a fashion designer when she grew up. Claudia also loved to write letters to her older brother who was away at college.

Sammy, also a Caucasian girl, loved to read and would choose to read every minute of the day if she could. One of her favorite activities was to curl up in bed with a good book and "lose" herself in the story. Sammy approached literacy tasks with great enthusiasm and loved to expand her imagination when working with her friends on projects and writing stories. She was an avid sports fan and athlete who participated in such events as soccer, gymnastics, and horseback riding. She regularly read books that gave her tips on how to improve her skills. Sammy was the oldest of three children and enjoyed reading to her younger brothers. She eagerly participated in the fifth-grade spelling bee, and much to her surprise, she won.

Lerissa, a multiracial Caucasian and Asian girl, was a "social butterfly" and loved to read most everything, especially biographies to learn more about other people. She was passionate about animals and hoped to work with animals at a zoo or marine park together with Sammy when they were older. She wanted to learn about everything so she would be really smart when she grew up, but not "nerd smart." Although a voracious reader and writer, math seemed to be confusing and frustrating to her, especially the more complex problems. Lerissa's parents were divorced and she and her brother split time between both families.

Anneka, an African American girl, was incredibly articulate and was considered to "know everything" by her classmates. Anneka was a precocious student and possessed an immense amount of world knowledge. She was rather mature and wise beyond her years. She was advanced in many subject areas, specifically math, and she received supplemental work from the teacher, which Anneka thought was easy. Anneka also participated in the fifth-grade spelling bee and was not intimidated by the older students. She delighted in reading stories about girls in past centuries or in the present time, but not "in the middle," and she enjoyed books that had main characters facing real-life problems. Anneka explained that she "really gets into the books and then I sort of feel really, really, really scared." She also revealed that she liked to exchange places with the characters and sometimes she could "feel" some of the accidents happening to the characters in the story. She was quite confident in herself and was a wonderful resource of information for her friends and classmates. Anneka had two older brothers who were very studious and proved to be good role models for her.

Getting to Know the Fourth-Grade Readers

Jane and Kathy cotaught fourth grade in a working-class suburban community on the east side of San Francisco Bay. Students at Henderson Elementary, a K–5 school with approximately 350 students, reflected the diversity of the neighborhood and community in which the school is located. The cultural diversity in the classroom included 66% Caucasian/non-Hispanic, 10% Asian, 13% Hispanic, 7% African American, 2% other, and less than 1% Asian Pacific or Pacific Islander. Ten percent of the students reported English as a second language on school documents and records.

When the school year began, Amy asked all 29 students in the class if they would be interested in reading a book and talking about it with other students. Each student completed a questionnaire that further identified those who most likely would be willing to share their interpretations and understandings about a story with others. Seven students indicated high levels of interest and agreed to participate. These seven students (five girls and two boys) became the group that Amy closely observed during the language arts period of the day. Five of the children were Caucasian, one girl was African American, and one girl was a multiracial mix of Asian and Hispanic. Academically and socially, the students exhibited a wide range of knowledge and abilities. Two children struggled to read with ease, while the other five had few difficulties with text. Some students were exuberant, imaginative, and full of energy; others appeared more reserved and unsure of themselves.

Kelly, a multiracial Asian-Hispanic American girl, was a thoughtful and engaged reader. She readily offered her interpretations and ideas about the story being read and discussed. During literacy events when the teachers assigned activity sheets to be completed, Kelly's determination to complete the task was evident. She quickly started the assignment at hand, concerned that she followed directions accurately. She worked hard to be perceived as a "good student." Kelly was not intimidated to challenge others to support their own interpretations during discussions. She frequently wanted to know how her friends arrived at various statements. Kelly also talked often of her grandmother, who lived with the family.

Marcy, a Caucasian girl, was also an interested and engaged reader. Her participation in the discussions, however, was much different than Kelly's. She seemed to have a "dreamy" quality about her. Marcy was very soft-spoken and often not heard by others when expressing her point of view. She regularly had to repeat her comments, or in many cases, group members talked right over her. During classroom events, Marcy did not volunteer answers or responses. She rarely raised her hand, and when called on, she stumbled as if surprised to be asked a question. It appeared as though she was not prepared with an answer, when in many cases it was more a case of her being intimidated by the whole-group setting.

Michelle, a Caucasian girl, was an accomplished reader, but she did not offer her ideas unless asked. She was somewhat of a perfectionist in her creation of products to submit to the teachers. Much of her time was spent on handwriting to ensure it was easy to read. Michelle interacted well with everyone in the classroom and was quite popular among her peers. She frequently talked about her younger sister who was learning to read. Michelle attended GATE (Gifted and Talent Education) classes one afternoon a week. When she worked with others, she did not hesitate to tell them what to write or where it should be placed on the page. Michelle's reservations to participate were most evident during the book club time when the discussion was free-flowing and less directed.

Elaine, an African American girl, was an enthusiastic reader who had difficulty in the decoding process. Kathy described Elaine as always wanting to work with peers, however, she was often reprimanded for talking during quiet times. She socialized with many friends on the playground. Elaine lived with her mother and younger brother. Although Elaine struggled in reading, she did not let it dissuade her from sharing her interpretations or offering suggestions to others. Her level of engagement was not reflective of her knowledge, but rather her social sense of what it meant to participate in discussions.

Robert, a Caucasian boy, also labored over the reading process and was viewed by the teachers as a struggling, reluctant reader. He was frequently absent, particularly on Mondays. Robert seemed to be raising himself. He lived with his mother and an older, high school-aged brother. Robert talked about "hanging out" with his brother and his group of friends. Robert's interpretations and insights often indicated a level of street-wise knowledge; he brought into the discussions a belief that if you did not look out for yourself, no one else would. When asked why the tribe in *Island of the Blue Dolphins* (O'Dell, 1960) was watching the Aleuts down at the shore, Robert responded, "to make sure they don't rip them off." He did not easily interact with others in the group, especially with Elizabeth.

Elizabeth, a Caucasian girl, was quite competent in reading and writing. She verbalized her ideas and interpretations freely, but struggled in her interactions with peers and the teachers. When attempting to have the teachers acknowledge her, Elizabeth often added the "oooh" when raising her hand, which seemed to backfire on her most of the time. She appeared to have a needy quality about her and was often denied requests to work with others in the classroom. During recess, Elizabeth usually hung out by the door eating her snack and not playing with other children. She was "talked to" on a number of occasions for what Jane and Kathy, the teachers, perceived as tattling.

Clark, a Caucasian boy, was the most energetic and imaginative of the group. He was a fluent reader, but had great difficulty working with others on any level. Clark completed his assignments and the readings at lightening speed with little regard for what the product looked like (unlike Michelle). His interest was in completing his work first. He did not want to be slowed down by his peers. Clark also made quick judgments about the viability of others' comments during literature discussions and would frequently tell them they were wrong. Although he did not have patience for his peers, they liked him and thought he was quite funny and quick witted. For example, he commented one day that he could not take his homework home because there was no more room in his backpack, which created laughter among those in the classroom.

Box 1.1 provides a reference chart of the students in each class. You may want to refer to this chart as you come to know these children through their conversations and stories.

Box 1.1
Focal Students in the Two Classrooms

Third Grade—Lynn (Mary)	**Fourth Grade— Kathy and Jane (Amy)**
Brandi	Kelly
Jennifer	Marcy
Rodney	Michelle
Tommy	Elaine
Claudia	Robert
Lerissa	Elizabeth
Sammy	Clark
Anneka	

Vignettes in subsequent chapters include students other than those highlighted in this section. The seven to eight focal students in each classroom that were most closely observed did not interact only with each other, thereby making it necessary to include other children's voices as well. Jackson is one student that began the year in Amy's focal group, but moved after Thanksgiving. He is present in many of the conversations, but not highlighted as a focal student. Other participants include Darius, Noel, Simon, Jessica, Brady, Daniel, Tony, Shawna, Bradley, and Tanner. Although their participation is minimal in most of the vignettes, it is important to acknowledge their contributions to the conversation or event.

Reflection Point 1.2

After reading our kidwatching notes and observations of students in these two classrooms, address the following questions:

1. What impressions do you have of your students?

2. Which ones seem to gravitate toward others and which students prefer to work on their own?

3. How might these observations help you make informed instructional decisions?

Who Are We and Why Are We Writing This Book?

This book reflects a collaboration between Mary and Amy. We are former elementary teachers with a vast range of experiences in many different types of school settings, from the urban centers of New York and Los Angeles, to the suburbs of Atlanta and San Francisco, and from kindergarten to eighth grade. We met while completing our doctoral studies at the University of California, Berkeley. It so happened that we began our dissertation work at the same time. We compared notes about what was happening in the classrooms we were studying, and often chuckled at the amazing stories our focal students shared, giving us a window into their world. As the days passed and we collected more data, we realized these teachers and students were struggling with some of the same tensions, albeit in completely different circumstances. How wonderfully strange this was. In our conversations, we reflected on our own teaching experiences in an attempt to find any correlation or explanation. Sometimes there was a logical explanation and other times there was none, which pushed us to expand our own definitions and understandings about teaching and learning.

Amy was interested in working in Jane's classroom because Amy and Jane were friends and colleagues from a number of years before when they taught at the same school in Los Angeles, California, USA. Jane had relocated to the San Francisco Bay Area and was teaching fourth grade at Henderson Elementary. Over the years, they remained in touch with each other, and at one point Jane indicated that she was interested in rethinking her literature program. She wanted students to make connections, to have the "lived through" experience that Rosenblatt (1978) talks about. After Amy had arranged to be in Jane's classroom, an opportunity came up that Jane wanted to take advantage of—job sharing. Kathy was a first-year teacher making a career change from the sciences. She had completed student teaching at Jane's school, so the two of them knew each other quite well. They agreed to split the week, with Jane teaching on Monday, Tuesday, and Wednesday and Kathy teaching on Wednesday, Thursday, and Friday. Additionally, Jane took the lead in language arts while Kathy was primarily responsible for teaching science.

Amy spent nearly 6 months in Jane and Kathy's classroom. She observed the 2-hour language arts period four mornings each week, and witnessed literacy events that ranged from SSR to literature discussions to comprehension and vocabulary tests. Amy was interested in how children participate in literature discussions, and she established a book club, in which a group of seven students volunteered to read and discuss a book they had self-selected. (See *The Book Club Connection: Literacy Learning and Classroom Talk*, by S. McMahon, T. Raphael, with V. Goatley & L. Pardo, 1997, for a detailed discussion of the book club research program.) The book club took place within the language arts time period, replacing the SSR time. Amy met with those in the book club to document the dialogue that took place. Informal conversations with the teachers at lunch and interviews throughout the 6-month period substantiated Amy's impressions and insights about the children, the tasks, and the ways in which they were responding to literature.

Mary's association with Lynn began when she phoned the principal of Eli Elementary, a local school where she had conducted previous research. She asked if the principal could recommend a teacher who was willing to allow a doctoral student into his or her class to conduct research for approximately 5 months. The principal highly recommended Lynn, a third-year teacher who wanted to have another set of eyes and ears in her classroom. Lynn was confident that she would enhance her teaching expertise from this experience. She strongly believed in creating a classroom community and encouraged her students to take advantage of the multitude of learning opportunities she offered. Mary arrived on the first day of school in late August and began observing and documenting what occurred in this classroom over the next 5 months. Mary visited Lynn's classroom 4 or 5 days per week. She observed math, social studies, science, reading/language arts, computer lab, recess, and occasionally lunch (where a great deal of literacy conversation took place). Mary began her research as an observer, but her role switched to a participant observer as she interviewed the children and sat in on their reading and writing groups.

It has been a few years since we observed in these two classrooms, yet we are still thinking, reflecting, and wondering about the events we experienced and observed. Amy currently teaches at Indiana University in Bloomington, Indiana, USA, and shares the stories of the teachers and children in our studies to highlight the complexities of literacy development with the undergraduate and graduate students in her classes. Mary is an educational consultant who works with teachers, administrators, and high-tech companies, and whose projects have been influenced by the findings from the two studies. We continue to be very interested in the ways in which children participate in socially mediated literacy events. We wonder if some of the literacy events would have been different if any of us had been cognizant of what we now call the hidden influences. Would we have changed anything about how literacy was enacted in the classroom? Would the tensions we uncovered reflect a different concern? Would the voices be different during the language arts time?

It is our intention and goal throughout this book to share treasured moments in the lives of the teachers and children we observed as they engaged in various literacy events. In these moments, we hope to share not only *what* was happening, but also some insight into *why* events occurred as they did. It is by examining the *why* that we can reflect and grow as teachers and researchers. We aim to contribute to the ongoing conversations about education in general and literacy in specific. We are most interested in middle elementary grade classrooms, because in our experience, it is at this level that many of the hidden influences begin to play a significant role in literacy growth and development.

Research Parameters

While the focus of these two research studies was on the children's ways of engaging in literacy events, those events were influenced by the classroom structure Lynn, Kathy, and Jane constructed with and for the students. The teachers obviously played an important role in the ways in which the children constructed meaning within various literacy events. Throughout the studies, we informally met with the teachers and shared our thoughts and impressions with them, primarily to seek clarifications. It was clear from the beginning that the teachers allowed us to come into their classrooms hoping to shed light on some of their own teaching practices. Although this was not a formal collaboration (which requires equal participation in the study), it was a partnership based on the realization that we could all benefit from the conclusions and implications of the studies.

Both studies were qualitative in nature, meaning that our research was conducted in the natural setting of the classroom and the data collected in these studies were in the form of verbal descriptions, phrases, and illustrations rather than numbers. We relied on our own observations, field notes, interviews, and video- and audiotaped transcriptions to capture the literacy learning and the spirit of these classrooms. The Appendix provides a more complete description on the data analysis procedure for both studies.

Goals of This Book

The remaining chapters of this book will explore the various tensions and successes the three teachers and the various learners encountered during a wide variety of literacy events. To set the stage for exploring the multidimensional relationships among issues of stance, social positioning, and interpretive authority, Chapter 2 discusses the theoretical framework that shaped many of the literacy events in these classrooms. Following this discussion, we profile the classroom environments and structures that the teachers established for responsive and insightful teaching. We also share the unique aspects of these classrooms.

In Chapter 3, you will become familiar with the notion of teachers being more explicit in their intentions and purposes for literacy events. Vignettes will be used to exemplify the continuum of the literacy stance, from aesthetic to efferent. When stance for an event is articulated clearly, the responses and interpretations seem to be more aligned with the identified intentions and goals. Misalignment is possible when teachers and students have differing stances for the same event. Chapter 4 discusses how students position themselves within literacy events. We examine the criteria students used to evaluate the plausibility of working with each other, and we share strategies for better understanding these criteria.

With stance and social positioning as a backdrop, Chapter 5 addresses the ways in which teachers and learners establish interpretive authority and sources of meaning for a literacy event. We talk about the importance of enabling children to assume roles within literacy events that move them beyond being mere "responders." In other words, you will be introduced to a range of discourse roles that learners may assume as they negotiate and share understandings of text in small groups, as well as in whole-class discussions. Additionally, you will see how text, teachers, or peers may be perceived as authorities.

In Chapter 6, we widen our boundaries to consider new directions and influences on the meaning-construction process. We examine the tightly woven relationship of the hidden influences. As stance, social positioning, and interpretive authority are brought together, we expand the discussion to include possibilities of working with social issues texts and integrating technology in the teaching and learning process. In doing so, the idea of flexibility among these hidden influences emerges.

Chapter 7 revisits the hidden influences and the relationships that are forged among them. Finally, the Appendix presents the data we collected in our studies of these two classrooms.

We encourage you to reconsider your own positions on the tensions and challenges faced in your classroom in light of the ideas and insights presented throughout the book. It is our hope that the strategies and resources provided in each chapter will support new directions for effective literacy programs in the middle elementary grades. Building a literacy program that is responsive to the multiple voices and diverse needs in classroom communities provides access and power to all those participating. Moreover, examining the influential nature of stance, social positioning, and interpretive authority affords a more powerful lens from which to view the multiple ways that teachers and learners orient themselves to, engage in, and interpret classroom literacy events.

Reflection Point 1.3

If we are to discuss the hidden influences, it is important to be aware of the more visible and tangible aspects of your program. What are some of the visible influences on meaning making found in your classroom literacy events? In other words, what are the materials, activities, time frames, assessment, and grouping strategies you have in place?

This book is more than data from our dissertation studies; it is the story of how our views of teaching and learning have been altered by the lessons learned from these children. It is our hope that the teachers we worked with gleaned insights from our studies, and more importantly, from their own students. We also hope that you, too, will come away from our stories and lessons with new treasures. The children in Lynn's class occasionally asked Mary, "What are you doing?" Mary responded, "I'm writing a story about you." "Can we read it? Can we read it?" the children begged. As promised, this is their story.

Chapter 2

Possibilities in Two Classrooms: Literacy in Practice

Tommy, Simon, and Rodney furiously scribble down ideas for their science fiction story. Jennifer draws illustrations for her story as her friend, Vanessa, continually asks her what she is doing. Jennifer explains as she draws. Lerissa, Claudia, Sammy, and Anneka sit on the couch talking about ideas for their story. Lerissa takes notes as Sammy jumps up and down and twirls around like a ballerina. Claudia sketches a picture of an antique dress her main character will be wearing in the story. Anneka references a book in her lap as she contributes her ideas.

In another corner of the room, Lynn sits at a student's desk reading aloud with two students. Brandi is working on the computer, brainstorming ideas and experimenting with the paint-and-draw program to create graphics she wants to add to her story.

This is a typical day in Lynn's third-grade classroom where children explore, discover, and discuss literature in different group configurations. Some children talk, others listen, while still others draw or write. Some prefer to work alone; others enjoy working together in small groups or with partners. All of these children and their teacher are engaged in literacy events, constructing meanings, negotiating ideas, and creating new experiences.

In Jane and Kathy's fourth-grade classroom, literacy events occur in more structured and whole-class settings. On this particular morning, students have been asked to brainstorm literary elements for Otherwise Known as Sheila, the Great *(Blume, 1972). In this story, the main character, Sheila, learns about fears and friendships. Jane has hung large* sheets of butcher paper with the words setting, characters, climax, and conclusion and has asked students to generate ideas and phrases for these categories. She records their ideas on these large sheets of paper. The students will use this information to write structured book reports.

The activity continues to a second day, when Kathy focuses on the climax and conclusion of the story. Kathy has asked students to identify events in the story:

Kathy:	Okay, what else? Robert, what is another event?
Robert:	When Sheila gets caught playing hide and seek in the closet. [Kathy records the comment]
Kathy:	What else happened in this book?
Jackson:	Sondra got a rope burn on her ankle.
Kathy:	That's when she got caught in the milk door. We'll add it to this. [She adds idea to climax sheet]. What else happened in this story?
Michelle:	Mouse was hiding in the attic.
Kathy:	In the attic. In the book, it said she hid in the laundry shoot the last time and got into trouble for it. This time she is in the attic.
Darius:	Why did she get into trouble?
Kathy:	For hiding in the laundry shoot, and then she fell all the way down.
Michelle:	When she was in the swimming pool and Marty taught her how to blow bubbles in the water.
Kathy:	Good.

This particular exchange of ideas between Kathy and the students demonstrates how literacy events in this classroom are often whole-class or whole-group experiences. As Kathy and the students continue to identify events in the story, opportunities for meaning making become available. Writing the suggested events and other aspects on the large chart paper provides all of the students with a reference point when beginning their own book reports. Kathy and Jane want to facilitate comprehension and meaning making as children read and respond to various literature selections.

The teachers we observed put into practice many of the guiding principles and characteristics of social constructivism as they established the learning environment. In this chapter, we start with a discussion on literacy teaching through a social constructivist lens. We then share common characteristics that the teachers embodied through the instructional practices, decisions, and routines in their respective classrooms. In doing so, we hope to better understand how teaching, learning, and literacy were conceptualized for these teachers and how their decisions influenced the meaning-making process for children. While we share vignettes and dialogues that capture the overall essence of the classrooms, we recognize that literacy instruction is a complex process. The ways in which the classroom routines are portrayed are merely generalized patterns we observed and are not indicative of the total literacy program.

Reflection Point 2.1

Reflect on and write a description that characterizes the variety of instructional strategies you use in your classroom. In what ways are you responsive to your students' needs? Share examples with your colleagues.

A Social Constructivist Perspective on Literacy Teaching

When conceptualizing literacy through a social constructivist paradigm, we recognize the value and importance of social interaction and socially mediated literacy events. Such opportunities to share and negotiate new meanings of texts and experiences are reflected in the works of many scholars (see Bruner, 1986; Dyson, 1993; Rogoff, 1990; Ruddell & Unrau, 1994). Vygotsky (1978) suggests that learning is a social endeavor, and it is through our interactions with others that new understandings about the world emerge. Dillon (2000) discusses the social constructivist perspective when she addresses responsive teaching in the foundation book of the Kids In-Sight series. She also offers Cairney's (1995) important considerations about social constructivism and literacy. These points include the following:

- Readers and writers create meaning; they do not simply transcribe, summarize, or extract.

- The meaning readers and writers create is always greater than the written text's potential.

- No two readers or writers can ever read or write with the same level of engagement.

- Above all, meaning is relative, socially constructed, and relevant within the context of the purpose and relationships to which the reading or writing is directed.

Socially mediated literacy events encourage participants not only to interpret text, but also to interpret their own experiences with text and others. These understandings are also culturally embedded—shaped by beliefs, values, knowledge, and ideas shared by a group of people. As teachers and children come together in classrooms, they bring with them their own background experiences, previous knowledge, and ways of interpreting the world. These viewpoints and experiences are tied to and reinforced by our culture, community, and cultural patterns.

Interactions among teachers and students uniquely shape literacy events. These interactions with others reflect different types of apprenticeships, each one offering new insights into the meaning-construction process (Riordan-Karlsson, 1997). The apprenticeships may take the form of scaffolding or weaving. Vygotsky's concept of "zone of proximal development" (ZPD) suggests that the ZPD is the distance between what a child is capable of doing on his or her own and what the child may do with support from a more capable peer or teacher. Some have used the term *scaffold* (Wood, Bruner, & Ross, 1976) to describe the type of assistance to which Vygotsky is referring. Scaffolding involves a teacher or more capable peer offering assistance to the less able student as he moves from one instructional level to another. The children in Lynn's class often provided scaffolds for each other as they worked on the computer—

publishing stories, improving math skills, or learning new software programs.

Steven:	Hey, hey, Rodney, what do I do now? I am stuck here and I want to get to the next level.
Rodney:	Oh, okay, all you do is click on here; you have to get to the top. I'll help you with some of these questions.
Steven:	Thanks, I think I can do it, but just hang here and see.
Rodney:	That's 32 [answering the problem "8 x 4 = ?"].
Steven:	Yeah, yeah, I knew that.
Rodney:	Get it. Hurry up, before your time runs out!
Steven:	Oh, that's, that's, 40? [4 x 10 = ?]
Rodney:	Yeah, good job. Now wait for your score on this level, and you will go up to the next level.
Steven:	Thanks. You know I've never been on level four.

In this example, Steven was unable to reach the next level in the game without assistance from Rodney, who was considered an expert in this game. Rodney was scaffolding Steven while the interaction centered on the task.

In addition to the notion of vertical scaffolding (in which one is able to progress to a more complex level or idea with the help of a more experienced and knowledgeable peer or adult), researchers have also discussed the notion of horizontal support, or weaving (Dyson, 1990), wherein children learn to interconnect experiences and histories with literacy events through discussions with others. For example, when children sit at a table or at the computer and share thoughts, ideas, or pictures, they help each other develop their stories through horizontal support. In one conversation about *The Mouse and the Motorcycle*, the fourth graders wondered if the main character, Ralph the mouse, was like their peer, Clark. Kelly shared memories and wove what she knew about Clark and the character together: "I think he is like Clark.... They both like mischief.... Clark likes everything exciting and so does Ralph." Amy contributed to the conversation by weaving in more examples of how these two are similar, saying, "Yeah, I can see that. I remember how Clark was sharing with us how he wants to jump out of airplanes and ride motorcycles really fast. These seem like the same things that Ralph wants to do." This weaving is reminiscent of a to-and-fro process of building an interpretation.

The third-grade literacy club (Anneka, Lerissa, Sammy, and Claudia) also exemplified horizontal weaving. For example, one morning the girls began writing a story based in the 1700s, the same time period as *The Courage of Sarah Noble*. After talking about some potential story themes, they discussed their ideas with each other, seeking assistance and recommendations for names of their characters.

Lerissa:	What is your story about?
Anneka:	I want to be a girl who lives in Williamsburg, Virginia, with the colonial people. I just can't think of a name for my character.
Brandi:	She's copying from a book, the American Girl series!
Anneka:	No, I am not! I am just getting the ideas from it.
Sammy:	I can't think of a name for my character either.
Lerissa:	Why don't you use the name Olive Oil?
Anneka:	What? The story is not about Popeye!
Lerissa:	How about Sara, Plain and Tall?
Anneka:	No, I can't use that either!
Sammy:	Lerissa, what is the name of your character?
Lerissa:	I don't know. I am still thinking—any ideas?
Sammy:	What about Alice?
Anneka:	No, that is not old fashioned enough.
Sammy:	What about Megan or Phoebe?
Anneka:	No, I'll decide tomorrow. Thanks anyway.

These girls were weaving their literacy experiences and histories into the conversation, understanding the importance of name selection for the characters.

The relationships that teachers and students develop in the classroom influence the ways in which knowledge is shared. Teachers' responsiveness to children's questions and wonderings will often establish a learning context that honors and supports risk taking. Being mindful of the multiple possibilities that await any literacy event also is important to insightful teaching and learning. Courtney Cazden (2000) spoke of "adventurous teachers"—those willing to take a risk with their curriculum, their teaching, and their ways of understanding students' progress in literacy development. Box 2.1 provides resources on social constructivist theories for you and your colleagues to reference.

Box 2.1
Resources for Learning More About Social Constructivism

These references and resources contribute to our evolving understanding of social constructivism and encourage readers to reconsider their own instructional practices.

Bruner, J. (1978). The role of dialogue in language acquisition. In A. Sinclair, R.J. Jarvelle, & W.J.M. Leveet (Eds.), *The child's conception of language*. New York: Springer.

Bruner, J. (1986). *Actual minds, possible worlds*. Cambridge, MA: Harvard University Press.

Dyson, A.H. (1990). Weaving possibilities: Rethinking metaphors for early literacy development. *The Reading Teacher, 44*, 202–213.

Dyson, A.H. (1993). *Social worlds of children learning to write in an urban primary school*. New York: Teachers College Press.

Riordan-Karlsson, M. (1999). *Constructivism*. Westminister, CA: Teacher Created Materials.

Rogoff, B. (1990). *Apprenticeship in thinking*. New York: Oxford University Press.

Vygotsky, L.S. (1978). *Mind in society: The development of higher psychological processes* (M. Cole, V. John-Steiner, S. Scribner, & E. Souberman, Eds. and Trans.). Cambridge, MA: Harvard University Press. (Original work published 1934)

Wertsch, J.V. (1991). *Voices of the mind: A sociocultural approach to mediated action*. Cambridge, MA: Harvard University Press.

Wood, D., Bruner, J.S., & Ross, B. (1976). The role of tutoring in problem solving. *Journal of Child Psychology and Psychiatry, 17*, 89–100.

Reflection Point 2.2

Take a minute to reflect on and write down your own beliefs about literacy.

1. What ideas are important to you?

2. What instructional practices reflect these beliefs?

3. What risks have you taken with curriculum, teaching, or in understanding a student's progress in learning?

4. As you continue to read, think about what you have written. Are there places where your beliefs are changing?

With a social constructivist framework in place, we now move to thinking about how Lynn, Jane, and Kathy established their learning environments to reflect insightful and responsive teaching. What are the influential teaching qualities these teachers possess? There are three areas in which we believe the teachers demonstrated responsive teaching: providing for socially mediated contexts, focusing on personal connections, and implementing a variety of tools and structures.

Responsive and Insightful Teaching

The teachers in these two classrooms clearly possessed the qualities of influential teachers—using highly motivating and effective teaching strategies, helping students with their personal problems, creating a feeling of excitement about the subject matter content or skill area, reflecting a strong sense of personal caring about the students, and demonstrating the ability to adjust instruction to the individual needs of each student (Ruddell & Ruddell, 1994). Above all else, Jane, Kathy, and Lynn were teachers who encouraged students to express thoughts, understand feelings, and respect others.

When discussing her beliefs about learning, Lynn shared the following thoughts in a conversation with Mary:

> I think that learning is very important, and it never stops, and it's not something that these students will walk out of here and have everything they need from third grade. Whatever they get here is just a stepping stone to the next level, and even when they get out of school they are still learning. So I feel it is a continual process. I also think it is a really important process and I believe every student is fully capable of learning. They do it at different rates and they reach it in different ways, but they all have somewhere when they get that "ah-hah!" and they're going to learn what they need to learn.

Jane's teaching style echoed many of Lynn's sentiments in that she tried to instill in her students that they were in charge of their learning. Jane provided many opportunities for the students to work at their own pace, and she wanted students to learn how to work together in many different situations. Further information about the qualities of influential teaching can be found in the resources listed in Box 2.2.

Box 2.2
Resources on Influential and Responsive Teaching

Dillon, D.R. (2000). *Kids insight: Reconsidering how to meet the literacy needs of all students.* Newark, DE: International Reading Association.

Ruddell, R. (1999). *Teaching children to read and write: Becoming an influential teacher* (2nd ed.). Boston: Allyn & Bacon.

Ruddell, R.B., Draheim, M., & Barnes, J. (1990). A comparative study of the teaching effectiveness of influential and noninfluential teachers and reading comprehension development. In J. Zutell & S. McCormick (Eds.), *Literacy theory and research: Analyses from multiple paradigms* (39th Yearbook of the National Reading Conference, pp. 153–163). Chicago, IL: National Reading Conference.

Ruddell, R.B., & Kern, R.B. (1986). The development of belief systems and teaching effectiveness of influential teachers. In M.P. Douglas (Ed.), *Reading: The quest for meaning* (pp. 133–150). Claremont, CA: Claremont Graduate School.

The Classrooms: Socially Mediated Contexts for Learning

Literacy was a social affair in these third- and fourth-grade classrooms. The teachers were committed to many of the principles of social constructivism and worked hard to provide learning environments that responded to the needs of the children in their classrooms. Desks in both classrooms were arranged in groups of four to six to facilitate the children working together in small groups. There were also meeting places in the classrooms where the children could come together to discuss daily events and listen to stories read aloud. The library corners in these classrooms invited students to read and share. Lynn's room had a couch for students; Jane and Kathy had beanbag chairs. Students were able to find comfortable spaces to discuss books and gain new understandings. The Sustained Silent Reading (SSR) time was a time for students to read self-selected texts. In addition to the popular series Goosebumps, many students read about sports figures and pop singing stars.

Students in both classrooms were able to work with peers and in small groups on a number of different literacy activities. A regular activity in Lynn's classroom was partner reading, during which students paired with classmates to read and discuss the text. Lynn hoped new understandings would emerge as the two readers brought their own personal experiences and histories to this event. Similarly, in Jane and Kathy's fourth-grade classroom, the literature discussions and book talk events enabled students to gain new insights and understandings by listening and responding to others' points of view. For example, in the following exchange, the students contemplate the importance of a mahogany penny box in the story *Hundred Penny Box* (Mathis, 1975). In this story, Michael is a 10-year-old boy who loves the time he spends with Aunt Dew, his great-great-aunt. Aunt Dew has a special mahogany box that is a keepsake for her memories and stories. At this point in the story, Michael's mom wants to throw out all of Aunt Dew's old things, including her mahogany box:

Marcy:	You know when Michael wants to hide the hundred penny box in the closet with his other things, and he [Michael] said that if his mom takes the hundred penny box then [Aunt Dew's] life would be gone.
Amy:	I thought that was a pretty powerful statement that if anyone takes away her hundred penny box, they are going to take her too.
Marcy:	I think…
Elaine:	That's her whole life.
Kelly:	I think that is because it is so special to her.
Marcy:	Because it is something she has had for a long time.
Kelly:	Probably like when she was a little girl.
Robert:	She put a penny in for each year.
Amy:	I think that each…
Robert:	Probably like each penny for her life, for one year of her life…
Amy:	One year of her life and they all have significance.
Robert:	She's 100.
Marcy:	She's 100, and she has 100 pennies in the box.
Robert:	She puts one more in, and she will probably die.

Another example that demonstrates the socially mediated contexts for learning is one in which children in Lynn's classroom were encouraged to confer with a partner when answering daily board work questions. One day the math question read:

> If it takes three oranges to make a glass of orange juice, how many oranges will we need to make a glass of orange juice for everyone in our class? (1) Figure out the problem. (2) Write in your own words how you figured out the problem.

Sammy and Claudia worked on the problem together. Sammy first asked, "Okay how many kids do we have in our class?" Claudia looked around and counted the number of desks. "There are three groups of six and one group of five. That's 23 in all." Sammy replied, "Okay, let's start with 23 and times it by three, right?" "Yeah," commented Claudia. "Well, look right here, three times three is nine and three times two is six, it's 69." Claudia began to write her answer in her daily board work (DBW) journal. They both wrote down how they figured out the problem and drew pictures of the groups of desks and the oranges in their journals. Sammy whispered to Claudia, "Oh, I hope she calls on us today to go up and explain our answer." "Me, too," said Sammy. After comparing their explanations, they agreed they were fine, and they both pulled out their SSR books to read while they waited for Lynn to call the whole group together.

Lynn encouraged students to share their ideas with the class by inviting them to the overhead projector to illustrate or explain their answers. She welcomed many different responses and at this point emphasized the process rather than the product, which was reassuring to the students.

The literacy environments in these two classrooms provided many opportunities for children to socially interact with partners, small groups, and the whole class. The teachers' encouragement of interaction and dialogue was embedded in the nature of the daily literacy events. Each day brought discussions of literature, personal stories, and local news events.

Focus on Personal Connections

The teachers in these two classrooms recognized the importance of responding to the individual needs of the children. Lynn used a variety of teaching strategies, which enabled her to adjust her instructional plans to meet the needs of the individual students in her class. As she explained,

> There are certain students that I'll read aloud to more than others because I want them to enjoy a piece of literature as opposed to getting lost in decoding the words. I'll set aside something else for them to read when we are just doing skills and just getting through it, and trying to figure out what the basic words are and something that is more at their level. But when it comes to the literature we're doing, I want them to enjoy it and feel excited about it.

The teachers planned and implemented a reading and writing program that included trade books and related literacy activities. Jane and Kathy commented that in order for children to be engaged and motivated, the story line needs to relate to the children's lives. To further substantiate this belief, Jane selected stories with characters she thought students could identify with and relate to on a personal level. *Otherwise Known as Sheila, the Great* introduced readers to a 10-year-old girl trying to make friends in a new neighborhood. *Island of the Blue Dolphins* introduced students to Karana, a girl struggling to survive on her own. Both of these stories had children as the main character. Additionally, Jane wanted to integrate social studies with her language arts program. Reading *Island of the Blue Dolphins* provided students with knowledge and information related to California history and geography, part of the social studies curriculum in the fourth grade.

The teachers had well-stocked classroom libraries that contained a number of titles for different reading levels, genres, and interests. The libraries were open to students at all times. Books were displayed in round carrels and on the tops of shelves. Children could leisurely peruse the titles when looking for a new book to read during SSR time.

The literature discussion time in Jane and Kathy's classroom served as an opportunity to hear how children constructed meaning and understandings. (See Box 2.3, page 32, for more information on how to organize and orchestrate literature discussions in your classroom.) Jane and Kathy met with all the students each day. This was an important instructional decision. They wanted to have a good sense of their students' reading abilities and felt it was necessary to listen to them read on a regular basis. They assisted children when difficult or unknown words appeared. On one particular morning, Kathy initiated a discussion related to vocabulary words for *Island of the Blue Dolphins*. In this discussion there were frequent opportunities to share personal connections and experiences. Tapping into prior experiences helped to clarify the meaning of words.

Kathy:	Noel, what vocabulary word did you define?
Noel:	*Dunes*—a hill or ridge of sand.
Kathy:	Everyone know what dunes are?
Robert:	Like little mountains.
Jackson:	Mountains of sand.

Kathy: Where have you seen them? Kelly?

Kelly: On the beach.

Kathy: Where near here do you see them?

Robert: Sacramento.

Kathy: Not far away.

Robert: Lake Tahoe.

Kathy: Near the ocean.

Jackson: Monterey. I just went down to Monterey to see the Indy race, and we saw a bunch of them by the ocean.

Kathy: They had dunes on the Island of the Blue Dolphins. Where did the battle take place? On the dunes—remember, they were hiding behind the dunes?

Kathy believed the vocabulary discussions were an important part of understanding the story, and she worked hard to make these discussions meaningful, because in her words, "There are a lot of vocabulary words they [the students] don't understand. They don't relate unless you have vocabulary [discussions]."

Box 2.3
Aspects of Effective Literature Discussions

Consider group sizes and strengths. Four to six students in a group is ideal for everyone to have an opportunity to share interpretations. Also consider the strengths each individual brings to the discussion. Some are better readers of the text; others have a better sense of how to manage and negotiate conversations.

Take into consideration the literature selection for the discussion. The story should be rich in details, characters, and plot. Stories that address issues of social justice and equity, the *social issues* genre, encourage thoughtful comments and responses.

Have students come to the discussion ready to participate. To help them focus on their ideas, you may want to have them write in a journal for a few minutes prior to the conversation.

Support students as they share personal and related experiences. What connections can the teacher make to facilitate more interpretive responses?

Review aspects of effective conversations, such as how to "share the floor," listen to others, and consider alternative points of view.

Implementing a Variety of Tools and Structures

There were many indications that the classrooms belonged to the students. Both teachers displayed much of the children's current work so that they would have opportunities to learn how others in the classroom approached the activity. In Lynn's classroom, "Math Graphs" displayed colorful graphs completed by pairs of children using a computer software program. The graphs depicted the results of surveys that the partners had conducted among their family members on a variety of topics, such as favorite kind of music, favorite pizza toppings, and the number of animals in each household. "Our Community" displayed a description of their community accompanied by hand-drawn maps. "Commonly Misspelled Words" was a list of words compiled by the whole class that were often misspelled in their written stories. Finally, a full-length bulletin board, "Eli's Museum of Modern Art," displayed self-portraits painted by each student.

In Jane and Kathy's classroom, a bulletin board displayed the children's work that related to the literature selection currently being read. The large windows served as wall space to hang student-authored stories about Halloween and Thanksgiving. The chalkboards at the front of the room informed students of schedules, work to be completed, and spelling lists, and often held a few comprehension questions related to the current literature selection. Side bulletin boards reminded students of classroom procedures and common grammar and math rules.

The teachers' instructional decisions reflected their knowledge of the importance of using a variety of approaches and tools to facilitate learning. Lynn used an integrated approach to learning and the literature-based reading program was her springboard. Each literature selection was cross-referenced to other curriculum areas, such as science, math, and social studies. Technology was effectively integrated into her curriculum, as well. Lynn often used a myriad of highly motivating comprehension strategies such as Directed Reading-Thinking Activity (DR-TA), Directed Listening-Thinking Activity (DL-TA), reciprocal teaching, group mapping activities, literature response journals, and K-W-L charts. Box 2.4 (see page 34) briefly explains each of these strategies.

Lynn varied the reading and writing activities within her class across content areas and even between her two reading groups. For example,

---

Box 2.4
Effective Comprehension Strategies in Literacy Instruction

• Directed Reading-Thinking Activity (DR-TA) and Directed Listening-Thinking Activity (DL-TA): The DR-TA and DL-TA encourage learners to make predictions based on background knowledge and experiences and then to evaluate their predictions after reading the text selection (see Stauffer, 1976). Students are asked to predict, analyze, and assess information, which are all critical thinking skills.

• Read-Aloud: Teachers and students come together to hear a story. The teacher usually reads the story and facilitates a follow-up discussion.

• Reciprocal Teaching: Reciprocal teaching involves four comprehension strategies: prediction, questioning, seeking clarification, and summarization (see Palinscar & Brown, 1984). The teacher models these strategies on a text passage; then students practice the strategies on the next section of the text as the teacher tailors feedback to each student through modeling, coaching, hints, and explanation. Responsibility for discussion gradually shifts from teacher to student.

• Group Mapping Activities (GMA): The GMA strategy asks readers to create a graphic representation illustrating their interpretations of the relationship between ideas and concepts (see Davidson, 1982). This representation takes on the form of a map or diagram.

• Literature Response Journals: Literature response journals provide a space for readers to demonstrate a range of responses including personal reactions, summaries, and understanding of the author's craft.

• K-W-L Charts: K-W-L charts encourage readers to consider what they already know and what they want to learn as a result of reading about a particular topic (see Ogle, 1986). A chart is constructed to represent K (what do I already *know* about the topic?); W (what do I *want* to know or learn about the topic?); and L (what did I *learn* as a result of reading or studying the topic?).

---

when the class was reading *The Courage of Sarah Noble,* the students wrote in a literature response journal after partner-reading each chapter. On another occasion, after reading the fairy tale *Puss in Boots* (Perrault, 1983), the children participated in a group mapping activity and subsequently wrote their own fairy tales. Additionally, Lynn used the DL-TA strategy when she read *The Cricket in Times Square* (Seldon, 1970) and *Stuart Little* (White, 1974) to the whole class during read-aloud time.

"Local News Report" was another literacy activity the third-grade children enjoyed. Once a week, a small group of children was asked to select an article from a local newspaper and share it with the class. They wrote a summary of the article, including why they chose to share it with the class and why it was important to the community. Following the presentation, there was an opportunity for discussion. The event became especially important during the social studies unit on "Our Community."

Jane and Kathy's fourth graders also participated in a variety of literacy events that made up the language arts program. For *Otherwise Known as Sheila, the Great,* students wrote book reports and drew pictures of what they imagined Sheila's bedroom to look like. The book reports are an example of the structured writing events in this classroom. Jane and Kathy provided the students with a format for completing the book report, which included Characters, Setting, Event I, Event II, Event III, Climax, and Conclusion. As with many of the writing events assigned in class, most of the writing was to take place as homework. Students drafted their ideas as "sloppy copies," which were later transferred to the book report form. The teachers wanted the book reports to hang on the back wall in time for Open House. The children considered this an important activity and completed it prior to the due date. They worked very hard on their reports, drawing detailed pictures and focusing on the neatness of their handwriting.

Literacy events related to *Island of the Blue Dolphins* included participating in literature discussions, creating a vocabulary wheel, completing comprehension skill sheets and end-of-chapter tests, making travel brochures, drawing a picture of the island, writing letters to Karana, and writing summaries of chapters. The vocabulary wheel, which consisted of a number of words and definitions, was displayed on the wall as a reference point for students as they read the chapters. The travel brochures and letters to Karana enabled the students to bring in their own understandings of the texts and develop their creativity.

Through the use of a variety of teaching strategies, tasks, and events, the teachers created a literacy program that responded to the many needs of their students.

*Reflection Point 2.3*_____

1. Draw a map of your classroom, and then describe how your learning environment helps or hinders your students' learning.

2. Does the physical set-up of the room encourage collaboration and social interaction?

3. Do children have a reading area or writing center where they can develop their literacy skills, individually or with others?

Unique Components Within the Classrooms

The similar responsive teaching qualities these teachers embodied contributed to the children's learning and meaning-making process. There are, however, other factors unique to each of the classrooms, such as technology, alternative schedules, shared contracts, and book clubs.

Technology

Technology was very much a part of the school culture and the children's lives in Lynn's classroom at Eli Elementary. In a conversation about favorite things to do in the classroom, Jennifer exclaimed, "I just love to work on the computer—it's one of my favorite things in the whole world!" Brandi echoed these sentiments and added, "I like to write stuff on the computer." These third graders had been exposed to computers since kindergarten, and at an early age they were introduced to keyboarding and other basic computer skills. There were two computer labs in the school, as well as three computers in each classroom. The faculty at Eli was committed to writing grants and securing funds to improve student achievement levels with the implementation and curriculum integration of technology.

In Lynn's class, the children used the computer, printer, and video camera as learning tools. For example, many students used the word-processing program to write their stories, poems, or plays, and then added graphics with a paint-and-draw program. Computer games such as *Math Mazes*, *Treasure Math Storm*, and *Where in the World is Carmen Sandiego?* were favorite "free choice" activities. Other programs such as *KidPix* and *KidPix Studio* were popular for adding illustrations to students' work. There was a steady waiting list for the computer area throughout the day, and this area generated a great deal of discussion, negotiation, and friendly competition between students. Additionally, a video camera was used to record various literary performances, including dramas and poetry readings. Children assumed roles such as director, camera person, and producer. Thus, the video camera was both an assessment and instructional tool.

Alternative Schedule

Due to the emphasis on technology use in her school, Lynn was fortunate to have her reading/language arts block follow a schedule that effectively met students' learning goals. On Monday, Tuesday, Thursday, and Friday, the class was divided into two reading groups; Wednesday was early dismissal at 1:00 p.m. for staff development. On a typical day, the entire class came in from recess at 12:30 p.m., and Group 1 immediately left for the computer lab. Group 2 remained in the classroom and had its reading/language arts lesson. Therefore, Lynn had 45 minutes with each group (half of her class), while the other group was in the computer lab working with a computer teacher. Lynn coordinated projects and assignments with the computer teacher so that the children had tasks to complete while in the computer lab. Usually the students worked on publishing a story or producing a graph for a math project. Sometimes the computer teacher introduced them to a new software program or helped them navigate the Internet. The coordination between Lynn and the computer teacher was an extremely important element in the success of her students' reading achievements and the integration of technology into the curriculum.

Shared Contracts

The shared contract between Jane and Kathy resulted in the two teachers negotiating how learning and literacy would take place in their classroom. They spent many Saturdays and evenings talking about and planning their curriculum, making decisions, and seeking advice about individual students. They decided that Jane would make most of the long-range curricular decisions regarding reading and language arts. Jane often played a mentoring role to Kathy when frustrations surfaced about how students responded to her and the activities she initiated. Kathy readily accepted Jane's suggestions and advice. The mentoring role that Jane played, however, often interrupted her own teaching practices. Jane did not feel as though she could give the children as much freedom as she had in the past during literature discussions and other literacy events, because she recognized that it would be difficult for Kathy to manage the class alone. Even though the idea of a shared contract meant fewer days or hours in the classroom, it was not uncommon to see either Jane or Kathy in the classroom on her "off" days, planning lessons, hanging up bulletin boards, or working with individual children. Together, the two teachers worked well in the classroom, complementing each other's strengths.

Book Club

The book club in the fourth grade occurred during SSR time and provided a group of students with opportunities to engage in conversations about literature in less structured formats. The group, led by Amy, met in the library, outside the classroom at a picnic table, or in the cafeteria, so as to not disturb the other students in the classroom. The children selected the literature, and by a majority vote, *The Mouse and the Motorcycle*, *Goosebumps: Night of Terror Tower* (Stine, 1995), and *Hundred Penny Box* were chosen. Each student had a copy of the story and often found places other than the local meeting spot to read. When in the library, students selected corners and read under the tables; when outside, they chose to sit under a nearby tree or by the bike rack. The cafeteria supplied many tables on which children could spread out their reading materials.

The book club context provided students with flexibility, not only in where they could sit, but also in how much was read and who they read with, if anybody. This flexibility was part of Amy's idea about what a book club might look like. Most of the students in the group chose to read with a partner. These partnerships were ever-changing, depending on who was present and who the students wanted to "hang out" with that day.

A routine was established for the book club. Students negotiated with each other about how much to read and when to have the reading completed. In most instances, students would read for a few days and then have a conversation. At first there was some concern about having everyone read the same amount, but that quickly disappeared when they agreed to not give away the story line. Michelle and Clark were two students that often read ahead of the group.

Tensions and Challenges in the Classrooms

The instructional decisions and practices in these two classrooms exemplify two learning environments responsive to the needs of the children. The teachers worked hard in each classroom to ensure meaningful and insightful learning events. They provided experiences in socially mediated events, and constructed a literacy program that aimed to focus on the students' own personal connections and their relevance to the story lines. In each learning environment, however, the teachers and students continued to struggle with the hidden influences that permeated many of the instructional decisions, and subsequently the ways in which the students responded. For example, the three teachers were not aware of their own stances toward the literature selections and what these stances meant in terms of literature discussions and assignments. Jane and Kathy's hopes for a literature program that attended to the reader's personal knowledge and experiences fell short when the focus was on locating "known" information in the book. This discrepancy had to do with the varied dimensions of stance, whereby the teachers' intentions and resulting activities were quite different.

Similarly, the influences of social positioning and interpretive authority were almost invisible to Jane, Kathy, and Lynn. The teachers were not aware of how children determined partners for literacy events, or how these decisions affected each child's social position in the classroom. Even when Lynn orchestrated the partnerships and collaborations, she did not consider the impact of social positioning on the meaning-making process. Likewise, the various discourse roles assumed in the literature discussions were not examined or considered necessary in the larger picture of the meaning-construction process. This may be due to the level of pressure felt, particularly by Jane and Kathy, to prepare students for state-level standardized tests and other district mandates. These teachers wanted their students to be ready for such events, and in preparing students for them, they may have been less cognizant of these hidden influences.

With the hidden influences identified and classroom context established, we focus in the next chapter on how important it is for us, as teachers, to be explicit about the purposes we set for literacy events with children. In other words, why are we planning and implementing various activities and tasks? We will also explore how explicitness of stance influences the types of responses and outcomes in a variety of literacy events.

Reflection Point 2.4

In this chapter we described Lynn, Jane, and Kathy's instructional approaches and structures and asked you to think about your own. As you continue to reflect on your style, what might be a personal teaching metaphor you would use to describe your instructional decisions, practices, and viewpoints?

Making Our Intentions Visible: Examining Explicitness of Stance in Literacy Events

On a November morning, the fourth graders are reading, talking, and writing about Chapter Three of Island of the Blue Dolphins. *Students have a series of comprehension questions to complete (such as, Describe the sea otter. Why did Karana worry about the sea otter? How does Karana know the men building the canoe were there to watch the Aleuts?). They have the option of working in pairs. Some choose to move to other places in the room to work with friends. There is low murmuring and whispering as the children work diligently on this task.*

After about 30 minutes, Jane calls the students together to review the questions and their responses:

Jane:	*Let's go to our story. How many of you have been to the Monterey Bay Aquarium? [A number of students raise their hands.] Okay. In the Monterey Bay Aquarium they have sea otters. What is one characteristic that describes the sea otter?*
Brady:	*Playful.*
Jane:	*Playful, okay. Tanner, one characteristic.*
Tanner:	*Small.*
Jane:	*When you think of small, show me with your hands what you are thinking. [Tanner holds his hands out to indicate a size about as big as two footballs.] Yeah, that's*

about the size I was thinking. Elizabeth, what is a characteristic?

Elizabeth: *Looks like a seal when swimming.*

Michelle: *Thicker fur than a seal.*

Jane: *Elaine, what's another characteristic?*

Elaine: *Playful.*

Jane: *We already said playful. We said thicker fur; we said swims like a seal. What else do you have?*

Brady: *Shorter nose.*

Jane: *Shorter nose. What about color?*

Jackson: *Whitish brown.*

Jane: *It's probably a lighter color on its tummy and darker on its back. Why would it be like that? Why do you think it is that way?*

Elaine: *The back is tanned by the sun.*

Jane: *I'm not sure about that. You will be studying about animal adaptation later this year. Number two, why did Karana worry about the sea otters?*

Jessica: *Worried about killing them.*

Jane: *She knows they [hunters] were killing them but she was worried about what was happening. She was worried that they would kill all of them. They were killing them one right after another. She was afraid eventually they would all be killed. It was like when you are worried about something and in the pit of your stomach, you are saying, "I don't think this is right." What other experiences have you had that are like that, where you were worried about something?*

Jackson: *When we went to L.A. with my dad—the gas was really low and we were in the middle of nowhere. We still had five more gallons, but I didn't know that.*

Elizabeth: When we went to Disneyland, there is one ride, the
Mountain one, and I was worried 'cause I didn't want to
go on it. Everyone was laughing [at me].

The conversation continues. Jane and the students make connections
to personal experiences and prior knowledge, which facilitates an understanding of the text and of each other. The experiences students bring to
the text support and enrich the meanings they are able to generate and
share. In this excerpt, we see Jane has been quite explicit about allowing
students to share personal stories. She asks them about a familiar and
rather famous aquarium, as well as a time when they have been worried
about something. The stories shared contribute to students' overall understanding about what the main character of the book might be experi-
encing or feeling.

On another crisp, sunny day close to Thanksgiving, the children in
Lynn's third-grade class run around the playground playing tag when
they hear the teacher call them. Quickly, they return to the classroom,
get a drink from the water fountain, and plunk themselves down on the
rug in a very tired fashion. Lynn begins a conversation with them by
asking, "What does the word giving mean to you?" Claudia quickly responds, "It's when someone is nice to you and gives you something."
Then Lerissa chimes in, "Yeah, like a friend or someone." "Or your parents," adds Sammy. After a minute or two of silence, Max joins the conversation with his idea, "I think it means giving up one of your toys to
your brother or sister." Rodney agrees and shares his own sentiments,
"Yeah, I have to give my toys to my little brother."

Lynn listens with a smile on her face, then asks the children, "What
are some other things, other than toys, that people give?" "Love," replies
Anneka. "Happiness and funny jokes," adds Velma. And Lerissa says,
"My brother tells me I give him a headache!" The whole class breaks out
in laughter—they can all relate to Lerissa's comment. Once they settle
down, Jennifer says, "I give my mom hugs and kisses." A pensive Tommy
then adds, "I guess I give help to others." Lynn exclaims, "Oh, that's
good. Today you are going to write a poem or a short story about giving.
Or you may try to define it in your own words. You can choose what to
write and how to write it. What does it mean to you? How do you

express it to others? Or how do others express it to you? Think about your responses in our discussion and what you heard from your class-mates. There is paper up here if you need some."

Following the discussion, Lynn is very clear and explicit with her intentions for the activity. The children respond well to this explicitness. Some children talk with their neighbors about the topic; others begin writing. When everyone is finished writing a draft, the class regroups and students volunteer to share their poems and stories. Generally the response is encouraging and positive. The children are excited to hear their classmates' poems and stories.

Reflection Point 3.1 _____

Recall a recent literature discussion or similar literacy event in your classroom.

1. Describe the event itself and to what degree explicit intentions and purposes were shared for the event.

2. Consider how this explicitness, or lack thereof, influenced the meaningfulness of the event for your students.

This chapter introduces the concepts of stance and explicitness. In the opening vignettes, both Jane and Lynn encouraged their students to bring their personal experiences to reading and writing. Jane commented to Amy one morning that she really wanted her students to understand Karana's triumphs and trials as they read *Island of the Blue Dolphins*. She hoped that if the students could personally relate to the attributes Karana exhibited, then they might be able to overcome their own personal diffi-culties and problems. Jane also wanted students to experience literature in pleasurable ways. Reading and writing were not only for information-gathering purposes, but also for expressing feelings and contributing to community building.

Although the vignettes reflect the teachers' explicitness in accessing students' personal knowledge and experiences, the influence of stance is not always prevalent or explicit in classroom discourse or in the assignments students complete. There are certainly times when teachers and students have a misalignment of stance or where they perceive texts and tasks differently. These moments can be disappointing and frustrating to both teachers and children. Meaning making is often jeopardized. Later in the chapter, we share some of these misaligned moments. Instructional strategies to minimize misalignments of stance are also offered, thereby supporting a more explicit and insightful way of teaching.

The Dimensions of Stance

Stance, as we defined it in Chapter 1, considers one's intention and orientation toward texts, tasks, contexts, and each other (Fish, 1980; Langer, 1995; Rosenblatt, 1978). The way in which a story is read is influenced by the literary stance a reader takes when engaging with the text. The way in which questions are asked and responded to is influenced by one's ideological stance, or one's beliefs about literacy. Simultaneously, the way in which teachers and children interact with each other is also influenced by the notion of contextual stance. Moreover, stance influences the decisions made about literacy environment, materials, and classroom community. Each of these decisions is related to dimensions of stance, which range from the ideological to the contextual to the literary/strategic (Flint, Lysaker, Riordan-Karlsson, & Molinelli, 1999). The interconnected nature of these dimensions implies that students' responses and actions toward texts, tasks, and each other contain traces of each dimension of stance (see Figure 1, page 46). For example, Lynn's structure for creative writing signaled to her students that this was a valued event, one in which opportunities to share ideas and write without worry were highly regarded. As she noted, "It's a chance for students to enjoy writing without worrying about spelling and grammar mistakes." Her own beliefs about literacy (her ideological stance), how she orchestrated events in the classroom (contextual stance), and her attention to what the purpose was for the text (literary stance) were in concert with each other as students accessed a variety of genres and partnerships in their writing experiences.

The ideological dimension exemplifies an individual's beliefs and ideologies about learning, teaching, and ways of being in the world. Ideologies

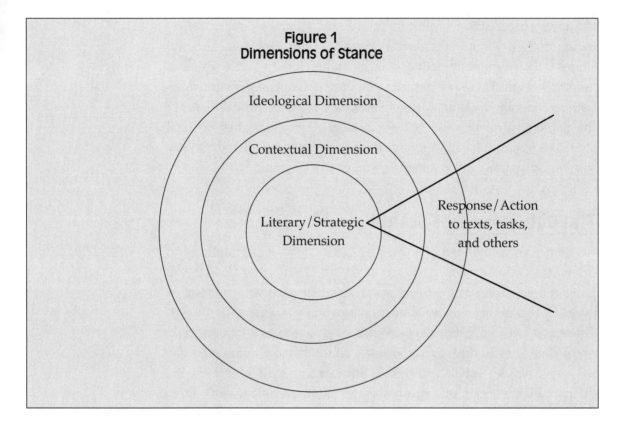

Figure 1
Dimensions of Stance

Ideological Dimension

Contextual Dimension

Literary/Strategic Dimension

Response/Action to texts, tasks, and others

are socially constructed and determined by people (Bloome & Bailey, 1992). Historical, social, cultural, and political identities are part of our ideological stance (Bakhtin, 1986; Beach & Anson, 1992; Davies, 1994; Kamberelis & Scott, 1992), and are shaped by past experiences, memberships in various groups, academic and professional preparation, and relationships with others.

The contextual dimension of stance represents the ways in which literacy events are enacted in the classroom setting—whether there are opportunities to work in partnerships or small groups, engage in collaborative and exploratory talk, or participate in more conversational literature discussions. The contextual stance shapes the local and immediate environment mediating the literacy event.

The literary/strategic dimension of stance centers on the reader's focus when reading a text. This focus is based on the relationship among purpose, intention or text cues, and response as reflected in Figure 2. In

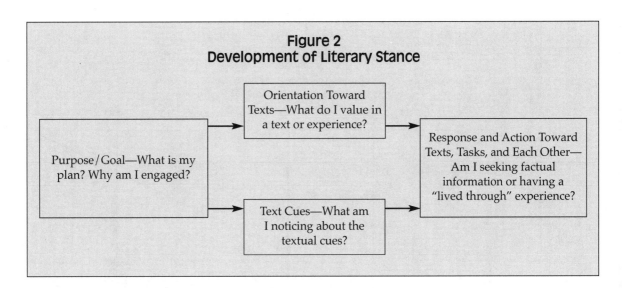

Figure 2
Development of Literary Stance

this diagram, the reader initiates the transaction with text by considering the purpose of the event. From purpose, a reader considers the orientation he or she has toward literacy events and the cues offered by the text, such as arrangement of margins, opening lines, and title. Purpose and text cues lead to responses and actions, which in essence reflect the literary stance the reader adopts.

Rosenblatt's seminal work in reader response theory offers a continuum of sorts, whereby a reader's intentions for a text may be positioned from predominantly efferent to predominantly aesthetic (Rosenblatt, 1978). When adopting a predominantly efferent stance, the reader focuses on the public and referential meaning—cognitive, analytical, quantitative, abstract. This stance may be evident, for instance, when a reader is trying to read the repair manual for a broken VCR player. On the other end of the continuum, the predominantly aesthetic stance focuses on the more private aspects of text—the emotions and images, the affective and sensuous ideas experienced in the reading event. Reading a novel on a rainy Saturday afternoon may engage the reader on a level of feeling like that of being "swept away." Figure 3 on page 48 demonstrates how aspects of meaning are attended to in different proportions depending on the stance (Rosenblatt, 1994).

The notion of a continuum suggests that as readers engage with a text, there may be a shift in focus or purpose, from efferent to aesthetic or vice

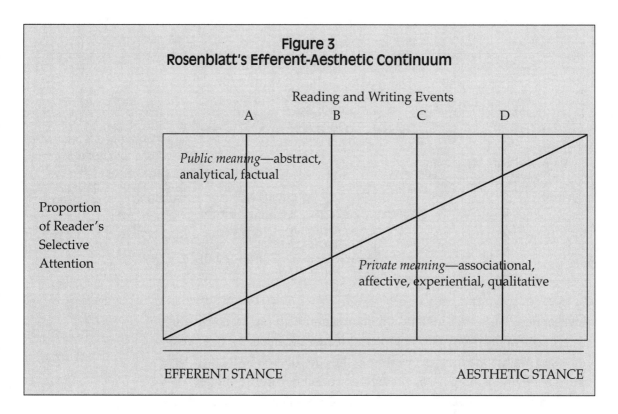

Figure 3
Rosenblatt's Efferent-Aesthetic Continuum

Reading and Writing Events

A   B   C   D

Public meaning—abstract, analytical, factual

Proportion of Reader's Selective Attention

Private meaning—associational, affective, experiential, qualitative

EFFERENT STANCE   AESTHETIC STANCE

versa. It also suggests that reading is not based solely in one orientation, but that a reader responds with more emphasis toward one or the other (hence, the use of the term *predominantly* in later discussion). Fluidity of stance is important to remember. As Lewis (2000) notes, "[Aesthetic and efferent] stances are not fixed, but instead are situated within the context of a particular moment, place, and set of readers and texts" (p. 257).

Aesthetic Literary Stance

Rosenblatt (1978) suggests that a predominantly aesthetic stance invites the reader to have "a lived-through" experience, which occurs when a reader attends to feelings, ideas, emotions, sensations, and images. It is the feeling of escaping into a text. Lynn shared her understanding of the aesthetic response when she talked with Mary about her reasons for using literature in her reading/language arts program:

> I think the aesthetic stance is where I stand often in our reading program because it is literature based. I am hoping that because of what we are

reading they [the students] are going to get that excitement about reading, that joy of reading; that they really just want to sit down with a good
book and read. Of course I want them to get the skills so they can do the
basic reading. As we all know, you need reading for all subject areas, so
being able to not just enjoy it, but know it is a tool, how to use it, it is a form
of communication, and it is a form of understanding. I think those are all
really important.... So how to do the basic skills, how to figure something
out on a page even if you don't know what it is. When it comes to our basic literature reading program I really want them to find the joy in it and
be able to imagine themselves there and see how it really is. Then it comes
to life.

From Lynn's perspective, it is important to seek enjoyment from the
text or experience. Recall the opening vignette of this chapter when she
led a discussion on the meaning of *giving* and how people show it in different ways. Through the discussion, she encouraged students to share
personal experiences and background knowledge as it related to the idea
of *giving*. Lynn's understanding of the aesthetic stance influenced the
students' responses and interpretations as they composed various pieces
of writing.

Technology also influences and encourages students' aesthetic stance
when writing. Many children in Lynn's class chose to publish their poems
and stories on the computer. In this respect, technology was used as a tool
to facilitate writing and, subsequently, meaning making. The computer provided children with autonomy to make decisions regarding not only the
content of their stories and poems, but also layout and graphics. In recent
years, Web sites where children can publish their writing have mush-
roomed, which further encourages aesthetic writing for children. Box 3.1 on
page 53 provides a list of sites to facilitate children's writing on the Web.

Following are the poems and writings of Tommy, Claudia, and Anneka. The concept of giving was an important issue for these three students, and a great deal of thought went into their writing. Tommy's poem
(see Figure 4, page 50) cleverly illustrates his personal definitions and
understandings based on background knowledge and experiences. Claudia's story suggests that kindness and friendship were essential elements
in her definition of giving (see Figure 5, page 51). Anneka defined *giving*
in a more ethereal manner. She discussed her ideas with her friends,
Lerissa, Sammy, and Claudia, and they agreed that love was the supreme

Figure 4
Tommy's Poem About Giving

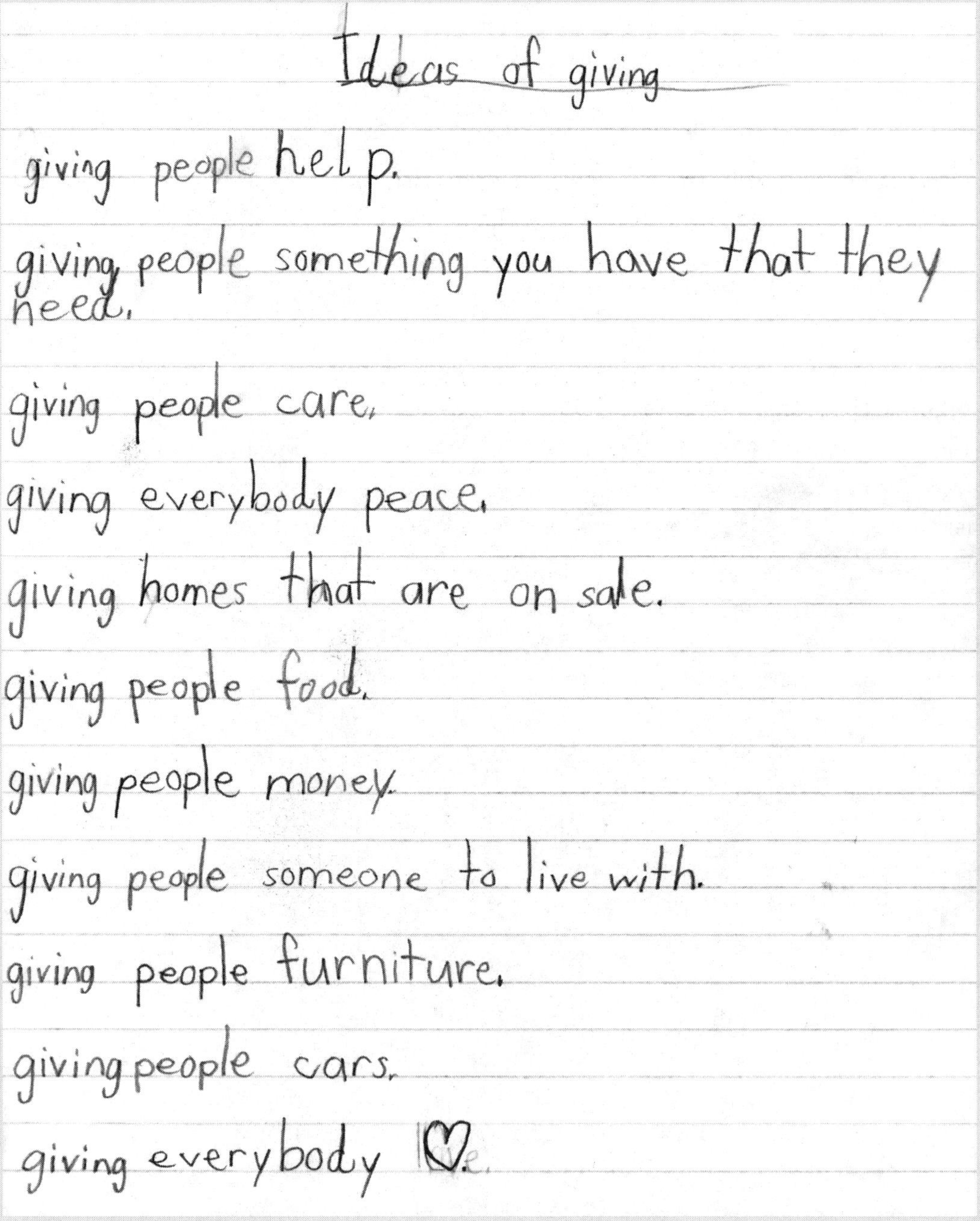

Ideas of giving

giving people help.

giving people something you have that they need.

giving people care,

giving everybody peace.

giving homes that are on sale.

giving people food.

giving people money.

giving people someone to live with.

giving people furniture.

giving people cars.

giving everybody ♡.

Figure 5
Claudia's Story About Giving

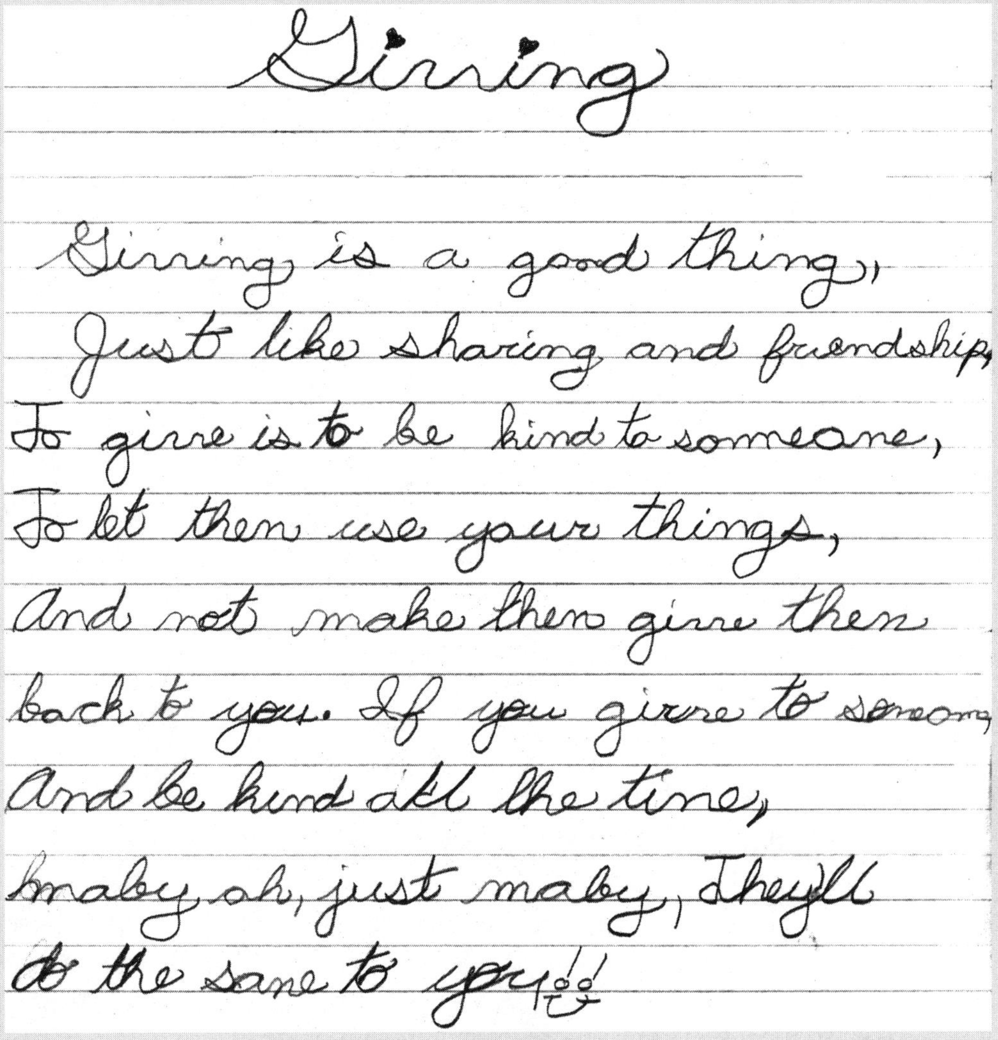

> Giving
>
> Giving is a good thing,
> Just like sharing and friendship,
> To give is to be kind to someone,
> To let them use your things,
> And not make them give them
> back to you. If you give to someone,
> And be kind all the time,
> maby, oh, just maby, They'll
> do the same to you!!

gift one could give and receive. Anneka's short story (see Figure 6, page 52) was expressive and descriptive.

As the students shared ideas, composed their pieces, and selected graphics to illustrate their writing, they were positioned along the aesthetic

---

Figure 6
Anneka's Story About Giving

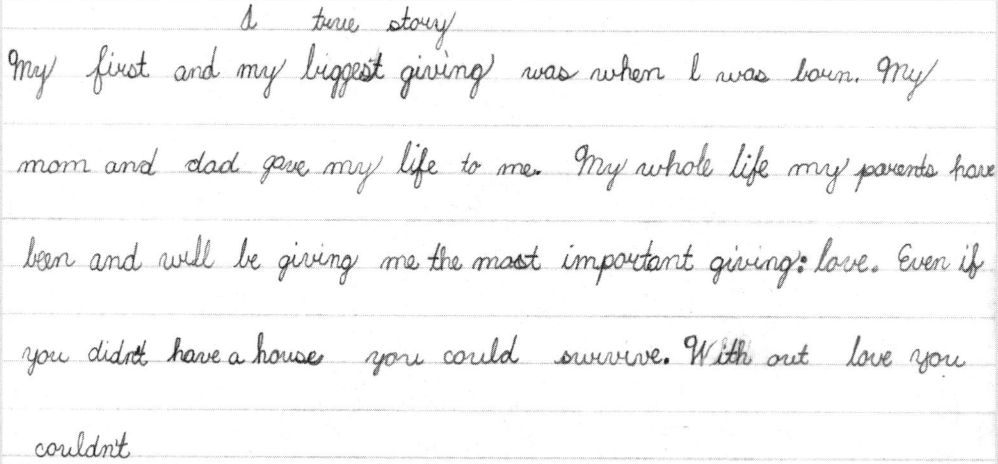

> A true story
> My first and my biggest giving was when I was born. My mom and dad gave my life to me. My whole life my parents have been and will be giving me the most important giving: love. Even if you didn't have a house you could survive. With out love you couldnt

---

end of the continuum. The enjoyment and personal connections the students made to better understand the concept of giving were evident in their presentations of the stories and poems. The "lived-through" experience Rosenblatt discusses can be seen in the images, sensations, and feelings these writers hoped to convey to their audience.

Lynn continued her discussion of the aesthetic stance by suggesting that responding from an aesthetic stance involves not only a personal response, but also a social, cultural, and political response (Lewis, 2000). She talked about how reading is more than enjoyment—it is a tool that children should know how to use, and it is a form of communication and understanding. These comments may be linked with Luke and Freebody's (1997) work on the social practices of reading and how reading should move beyond the personal to the critical. To do so involves "shifting attention from comprehending, analyzing, or interpreting literature texts to reading life through texts and texts through life" (McGinley et al., 1997, p. 63). From an aesthetic stance, readers can examine the social, cultural, historical, and political construction of texts, tasks, and contexts.

Box 3.1
Publishing Children's Work on the Internet

These pages are multilingual, multiage, multicultural, and multidisciplinary.

Global Story Train—storytrain.kids-space.org
Story Train is an illustrated, collaborative story project for creative children. It began in July 2000 as a sister project of Vote, supported by the Japanese Ministry of Posts and Telecommunications, the United Nations, and many other organizations, to encourage a global and multicultural learning experience for children.

Inkspot—www.inkspot.com/young
Inkspot is an award-winning resource and community for writers of all ages and levels of experience. At this site, young writers can chat with their peers, publish their work, and learn creative Internet strategies to advance their writing careers. Students can access useful tips and advice, including interviews with professionals in the field; they can locate writing links to help them get started as young writers; and they can learn about associations, workshops, and writing groups to join.

International Kids' Space—www.kids-space.org
Kids' Space is a commercial-free Web site that offers creative activities for children, communication activities (such as penpals), and the Guide Bear's tour as a tool for using the site and teaching about technology. In the Kids Gallery, children can exhibit their artwork, and in the Storybook section, children can write, read, and send their stories to other children. In the Beanstalk section, a child can cooperate to create a picture book on the Internet by sending either a picture or a story that goes with another child's work. In the On Air Concert section, children share and play musical works they have created.

KidLink—www.kidlink.org
KidLink is a nonprofit, nongovernmental, humanitarian grassroots organization that works to help children and youth to become involved in a global dialog for personal networking. KidLink offers mailing lists, discussion groups, art exchanges, special programs, and joint projects for students.

TeenLit.com—http://www.teenlit.com
The sole purpose of TeenLit.com is to promote teen literacy by providing a forum for teen writers to publish and discuss their writing and review and discuss books they read, and by providing a resource for their teachers.

This broader notion of aesthetic stance is exemplified in conversations during the book club experience in Jane and Kathy's classroom. When Amy initiated the book club, her identified purpose was to read and discuss literature by examining the personal and social connections. Frequently, the children escaped into the story line, wondering about character actions and how they would have reacted given the same circumstances. In the following excerpt, the students are discussing events in Chapter Five of *The Mouse and the Motorcycle*, in which Keith has given Ralph the motorcycle to ride:

Elizabeth: How can the motorcycle go when there is no motor on it?

Kelly: Because the boy already told him.

Clark: Because it is a magical moment.

Elaine: It's make believe. It's not a true story.

Elizabeth: Yeah, but if it was true, how could it go?

Kelly: It's fiction.

[Students begin to talk all at once, which makes it difficult to decipher and understand. The topic then moves to what Marcy thinks about being a mouse.]

Marcy: What I would like to do is be a mouse because you can go into other people's houses and get in there.

Robert: The bad thing…

Elaine: I know…

Elizabeth: The bad thing…

Clark: The bad thing is they spray poison in the house when they are gone and they kill the mice.

Elizabeth: Another bad thing about being a mouse…

Elaine: If you get caught…

Elizabeth: No, if you, if you're a mouse living in an apartment or hotel, you won't get to go anywhere. You have to stay in the hall.

In this interchange, the students pondered the viability of a motorcycle being able to move without a motor, as well as what their life might be like as a mouse roaming the hallways of a hotel or apartment. With a predominantly aesthetic literacy stance, they addressed both personal and social connections by talking about how humans view mice as something to exterminate.

Efferent Literary Stance

On the other end of the continuum is what is known as a predominantly efferent stance (Rosenblatt, 1978). This stance is one of locating information within the text. An efferent stance is most commonly adopted when the reader is trying to gain information about a particular process, event, or concept. Rather than focusing on the "experience" that is being lived through, the efferent stance focuses on what can be carried away from the text. Readers tend to adopt efferent stances when researching text for particular kinds of information. Lynn's third graders researched a candy factory using the Internet prior to taking a class trip. They wanted to find information about the factory, including location and directions to the site, hours, and tour information.

Similarly, a predominantly efferent stance may be adopted when teachers and students selectively attend to the literal details of the text, such as characters' names, progression of events, or where the story takes place. For example, when Kathy and the fourth graders reviewed the sequence of events for *Island of the Blue Dolphins*, their purpose was to complete a skill sheet that focused on naming characters, identifying the setting, and labeling some of the conflicts and resolutions. The responses valued in this exchange were those that accurately reflected an understanding of the sequence of events, rather than a personal, social, or political interpretation.

Kathy:	What was the problem with the main character? What did she have to overcome? What was the conflict?
Clark:	She was stranded.
Kathy:	She was stranded. She was left on the island all by herself.
Kelly:	She was stuck on the island. [Kathy refers to the directions on the skill sheet.] Look at these. They are not in order. What happens before Karana is stranded?
Clark:	Jumped off the boat.
Kathy:	What happens first?
Clark:	Ship comes in.
Kathy:	What happened first?
Kelly:	Oh, I forgot. I don't know that word [pointing to the word *rescued* on her skill sheet].
Kathy:	Karana is rescued. What is the first thing that happens?

Robert:	Karana misses the ship.
Kathy:	Karana misses the ship. That's the beginning of the book. So in the first spot [on the paper] you might have "Karana misses the ship." What happens after she is stranded? Look at your list.
Clark:	She starts harvesting stuff.
Kathy:	No, look on your list.
Clark:	Karana befriends Rontu.
Kathy:	Karana builds her house. Did she have a house built before she got the dog? Yes, she did. Aleuts slaughter the natives. That's the first one [again referring to the order of events on the skill sheet]. What ship did she miss? Not the first one, she jumped off that one.
Tony:	The second one.
Kathy:	The one that came much, much later. What happened after the Aleuts slaughtered the natives?
Clark:	If she didn't jump off the ship she probably would have died on the ship.
Tony:	Nobody can jump off a ship.
Clark:	Uh-huh.

Kathy's purpose and orientation to the literacy events signaled to the students that what was important was being able to correctly identify the series of events that took place. Her reference to the directions on the skill sheet suggested that she was reminding students of the stated goal. Kathy also initiated questions that required students to reflect on and recall a sequence of events in the story, and in doing so limited students' opportunities to bring in personal experiences or other related texts.

Intention and Types of Responses

Intention plays a pivotal role in the ways in which readers respond to texts, tasks, and each other during literacy events. Intention "functions as a mediator between attitude [purpose] toward reading and reading itself [response/action]" (Ruddell & Unrau, 1994, p. 105). During literature discussions and other literacy events these intentions become explicit through the types of responses constructed. To better understand the somewhat slippery nature of the literary stance, let us return to Jane and Kathy's room and another conversation about *Island of the Blue Dolphins*. In this discussion, the students have been asked to summarize Chapters 11 and 12.

Jane:	What can we say about Chapter Eleven?
Clark:	Ummm, she saw the house by the stone. She made a house by the stone.
Jane:	Well, did she make it then or did she…?
Clark:	She started getting the building materials.
Darius:	She decided on two places where to, um…
Jane:	She elected two possible places for a permanent home. What else can we say about it, Elaine?
Elaine:	Um, she moved her home by the wild dogs.
Jane:	Did she?
Jessica:	She moved it on a flat rock.
Jane:	But in this chapter, did she decide where she was going to put it? What was one reason she wanted West Lake? What was one thing she liked at that spot?
Clark:	Um…
Tony:	Forest water spring.
Jane:	Okay, with one location, the water was better, but that's where the…. Who was there that was dangerous?
Kelly:	The dogs.
Jane:	The dogs, but that is where the dogs were. Okay. The other spot was by the sea elephants. Chapter Twelve. What happened in Chapter Twelve? [At this point Jane reads a summary from the teacher resource book she has for *Island of the Blue Dolphins*.] What was Chapter Twelve about?
Michelle:	She started building her house.
Jane:	Right [starts to write sentence on the board—Karana builds her…] It is more than just her home because she did the whole area. What would you call that?
Tony:	Spot.
Jane:	Spot, I don't know.
Elaine:	Her village.

Jane:	Well, not really a village.
Shawna:	Area.
Jane:	That's closer. Karana builds her home and secures— makes safe—secures the area around it.

An initial analysis of this particular exchange suggests a somewhat limiting meaning-making experience if the focus is to build personal responses and connections. However, if we reframe the conversation and consider what Jane and the students selectively attended to in the text and conversation, we recognize Jane's intention of having students identify and recall information that was available in the text. Likewise, students constructed responses that reflected some understanding. Jane's use of the Initiate-Respond-Evaluate (IRE) discourse structure (Cazden, 1986; Mehan, 1979) enabled her to monitor the conversation as well as record particular ideas and comments.

Focusing on text-based meanings shapes conversation differently than when the intention is to share personal experiences and stories, as seen in the vignettes that open this chapter. Both stances contribute to meaning making. But what becomes important as teachers and students engage in literature discussions is the degree of explicitness in their intention toward texts, tasks, contexts, and the community in which the discussion occurs.

Misalignments of Stance

Teachers and students do not always read the cues set forth by purpose, orientation, or intention toward text, task, or context, resulting in what we call "misalignments of stance." These tensions often play out as differences and points of conflict in how readers interpret and respond to questions and ideas. At these moments, meaning making is jeopardized. Again, we return to the two classrooms to illustrate misalignments.

Jane and Kathy expressed interest in encouraging students to make explicit connections between their own lives and those of the characters about whom they were reading. For example, Jane commented to Amy that she really wanted students to understand Karana's triumphs and trials as they read *Island of the Blue Dolphins*. She envisioned reading and

writing as more than skills for information gathering, but also for expressing feelings and contributing to community building. These teachers
valued personal response, but this was not always apparent. In the following exchange, the purpose seems to shift without any explicit indica-
tors for the students to follow. A moment of tension results between
Elizabeth and Kathy, as Elizabeth tries to infuse a personal connection in
a discussion centered on other aspects of the story.

Kathy: Picture in your mind, what are you seeing?

Elaine: You see water and you see brown things in the water.

Kathy: So, what's the sea otter doing?

Elaine: Playing.

Kathy: Laying on its back, cruising around, laying there looking at
the sky. He's having fun; he's just playing there.

Clark: It's like he's playing, saying, "I don't want to be killed."

Elizabeth: When I went to Water World...

Kathy: Elizabeth, we don't need stories. We need to get this read.

Elizabeth: I saw a sea otter.

Kathy: At Water World?

Elizabeth: No, um...

Kathy: Marine World.

Elizabeth: Marine World.

As evidenced in this exchange, Kathy's purpose and intentions were
more along the lines of a predominantly efferent literary stance. She
wanted the students to construct an understanding about the sea otter
from the reading. When Elizabeth attempted to construct a response
more reflective of a personal experience, it was in opposition to Kathy's
orientation. A misalignment occurred, thereby potentially limiting Elizabeth's engagement and the overall effectiveness of the discussion toward
meaning making.

Misalignments do not always occur with students wanting to assume
a more aesthetic stance and teachers focusing on the efferent side of the
continuum. The book club experience demonstrates that misalignments are
possible in a variety of settings. As mentioned earlier in the chapter, Amy
facilitated this book club with the purpose of having children interpret

text from a personal and social perspective, more along the lines of an aesthetic stance. Michelle struggled in this context—she was rather silent and nonresponsive. When she did engage, many of her responses were factual in nature, thereby narrowing the ways in which she appropriated and interpreted texts.

Elaine: Yeah, when Keith took the motorcycle out of his pocket.

Michelle: No, it was Matt. Matt took the motorcycle out of his pocket.

Elaine: Oh yeah.

Michelle: 'Cause he had found it in the pile of linens and it's all chewed up.

Elaine: And Keith is like "Where did you find it?"

As the book club continued, Michelle's initial reservations became even more pronounced. She perceived discussions as opportunities to share known information, while her peers and Amy viewed discussions as opportunities to share personal insights and reactions. Again, a misalignment in purposes, orientations, and textual cues resulted, which disrupted the responses that were given and those that were valued.

In her third-grade classroom, Lynn established a partner reading structure in which students were organized in pairs to read portions of a literature selection as part of the language arts curriculum. Her goal and purpose for the event was to have students read and discuss a story, focusing on what they thought about as the story was being read. The students interpreted the event differently. For them, the purpose was to "read aloud." Students focused on who was reading what page and how much each one was reading, rather than talking or discussing various interpretations of the story. The discrepancy caused the teacher and students to lack a clear understanding or direction for the event, resulting in compromised meaning making.

Efferent and aesthetic literary stances are dynamic, which means that teachers and students may begin with one stance and later reconsider the ways in which they are reading the text. Lewis (2000) reminds us not to polarize the two ends of the continuum, but rather to consider the multiplicity and complexity of reader response. Box 3.2 contains a number of recommended sources to examine for more information and knowledge related to reader response and stance.

Box 3.2
Resources on Reader Response and Stance

These readings are recommended to expand your thinking about the influence of stance on the meaning construction process and to show you how to move toward planned, responsive pedagogy:

Flint, A. (2000). Escapists, butterflies, and experts: Stance alignment in literary texts. *Language Arts, 77,* 522–531.

Flint, A., Lysaker, J., Riordan-Karlsson, M., and Molinelli, P. (1999). Converging and intersecting views: An investigation of stance in four independent classroom studies. In T. Shanahan & F. Rodriguez-Brown (Eds.), *National Reading Conference Yearbook, 48.* Chicago: National Reading Conference.

Langer, J. (1995). *Envisioning literature.* New York: Teachers College Press.

Lewis, C. (2000). Limits and identification: The personal, pleasurable, and critical in reader response. *Journal of Literacy Research, 32,* 253–266.

Many, J.E. (1990). The effect of reader stance on students' personal understanding of literature. In J. Zutell & S. McCormick (Eds.), *Literary theory and research: Analysis from multiple paradigms* (39th yearbook of the National Reading Conference; pp. 51–64). Chicago: National Reading Conference.

Probst, R. (1990). *Five kinds of literary knowing. Report series 5.5.* Albany, NY: Center for the Learning and Teaching of Literature.

Rosenblatt, L. (1978). *The reader, the text, the poem: The transactional theory of the literary work.* Carbondale, IL: Southern Illinois University Press.

Literary stance plays a significant role in how participants engage in literature discussions, yet their orientations and intentions toward the text are generally not made explicit. Perhaps if teachers and students made their intentions public as they shared understandings, literature discussions may be productive, and ultimately, more meaningful.

Reflection Point 3.2

Make a list of the last three to five books or articles you have read.

1. For each selection, identify the literary stance you predominantly assumed for the text.

2. Speculate as to why you read those texts from that stance.

3. What might you gain by reading the text from a different stance?

4. Even when considering academic texts, what might come from an alternative stance?

Instructional Strategies That Complement Explicitness of Stance

Making public the reasons for engaging in a discussion is important to shaping the direction of the conversation. How might teachers and students talk about their orientations and intentions for participating in a literature discussion, whether it is a narrative or expository text selection? Possible avenues to encourage more discussion on stance include (a) opening up the discussion to address why people engage in the practice of reading, (b) writing in literature response journals, (c) examining texts after reading them, and (d) filling out comparison charts of the different kinds of questions that highlight different stances.

Inviting the Language of Stance Into the Conversation

Presenting the different ways in which a text can be read provides students with language to talk about how they entered the text. In other words, by making public the possibility of different intentions and purposes, students may come to recognize their own stances toward texts and how these stances influence their interpretations. Engaging in reflective talk about stance encourages participants to consider alternative orientations when reading and discussing texts. The questions in Box 3.3 provide a guide to support the conversation.

Literature Response Journals

Responding in writing to literature provides opportunities for children to write in an unstructured format about ideas, questions, and connections made while reading the text. The nature of journal writing focuses not on conventions and spelling, but on ideas and content. Some journals are personal and confidential between the student and teacher; other forms, such as learning logs or double entry journals, are intended for a public audience. Thought Ramblings (Pappas, Kiefer, & Levstik, 1999) are formats that encourage students to respond within 3 or 4 minutes to a question, statement, dialogue, class discussion, or reading passage. Literature response journals allow students to construct meanings based on

---

Box 3.3
Questions to Introduce Stance Into the Discussion

- Why do people read?
- When you read a story, what are some of the things you like to think about?
- It seems to me that many times we read things differently. Any ideas on why we might do that?
- Do you have books, magazines, comic books, or other texts that you read differently than the literature selection we are reading in class?
- What do you want to learn from reading this book? How does it challenge or complement what you already know?
- Are there other stories that remind you of this one? What did you focus on in those stories?

---

personal experiences with the text, while also supporting multiple stances and points of view.

To illustrate, on the first day of implementing the *Courage of Sarah Noble* literature unit, the students in Lynn's class made their own journals with colored paper covers and lined paper pages. They each decorated the covers in their own creative way. Lynn explicitly instructed them to partner read each chapter and then individually write an entry in their journal. The entry was to be written in the first person, from Sarah's point of view. Before they began to read, there was a group discussion about the assignment in which Lynn offered multiple examples of writing in the first person so there was no uncertainty when it came time to write a journal entry. Rodney commented, "It's gonna be hard to write like a girl. I don't know how a girl thinks." Lynn responded, "Think of it as a challenge." The students were instructed not to write a summary of the chapter; rather, they were given options. They could write a reaction to an event in the chapter, make a prediction of what might happen in the next chapter of the story, or continue a dialogue between two characters in the chapter. In addition to writing an entry for each chapter, Lynn encouraged them to draw an illustration to accompany their entry.

Although Rodney had thought it would be difficult to write from the point of view of a girl, in a relatively short amount of time he found it easy to trade places with Sarah and write about his feelings and anxieties in his journal entries. The following example is an excerpt from Rodney's journal:

Chapter Eleven—My Family

Father reternd [returned] today with my family. My little sister is walking she walkd [walked] into my arms. I told them about Tall John and his family and I told them the Indians are not savages! They are my new friends. I told them they do not have to be affrad [afraid].

Looking Backward

Lucy Calkins (2001) describes a method for interpreting text from the vantage point of its ending. This strategy helps readers to reconsider their understandings and interpretations in light of the particular stance adopted. Once students have finished reading a text selection, it is important to have a sense of the whole plot or theme of the story and how the details reflect the big ideas. In Box 3.4, adaptations have been made to Calkins's chart to better connect with the issue of stance.

Comparison Charts

Comparison charts document various questions that enable children to assume different stances. They can be used to encourage learners to discuss how the questions support or hinder various stances. As you ask

---

Box 3.4
Ways to Linger at the End of the Story

- Think about what the whole book is saying. One way to do this is to ask, "What single section best captured the author's meaning?" Another way to think is to ask, "How is the message of this book similar to (and different from) the message of another book?"
- How do the textual cues and elements of the text contribute to how you are "reading" the book?
- Think about why the author ended it this way. How might a different ending contribute to a different stance?
- Lay some of the books you know well next to this one. Did you read them with the same purpose and stance in mind? How are they similar; how are they different?

questions during the conversation, you may want students to indicate where a particular question should be recorded on the chart. By filling in the chart and talking about the nature of the questions, students will learn more about the issue of stance and how various purposes for the event signify and determine the types of intended responses. We have provided an example of a comparison chart for use with the literature selection *Island of the Blue Dolphins* in Figure 7 (see page 66).

Reflection Point 3.3_____

To make stance a more explicit part of your instructional planning and practice, implement one of the strategies just shared.

1. Why did you select this particular strategy?

2. Reflect on how your students responded to stance as an explicit and important element of the lesson.

_____

In this chapter we have explored the nature of stance and why making our intentions and goals for literacy events explicit is important as we unearth these buried treasures. Stance plays an extremely influential role in the meaning-construction process, affecting not only participation but the direction of interpretations. We demonstrated how explicitness of stance promotes effective meaning making, and we showed what happens when teachers' and students' stances are misaligned. The instructional strategies we presented are designed to encourage teachers to make visible how stance can shape the ways in which participants respond to text.

In the next chapter, we discuss the second hidden influence—social positioning. We demonstrate how literacy practices are socially mediated practices and how students position themselves within such events. Before you read on, jot down answers to the questions posed in Reflection Point 3.4.

Chapter 3

66

Figure 7
Comparison Chart for Chapter Two of *Island of the Blue Dolphins*

Efferent Stance	**Aesthetic Stance**
(carry away information)	(personal, social, political interpretations)
What does the word *league* mean?	Are you surprised at Chief Chowig for letting Captain Orlov change his plans? Why do you think this?
What are the Aleuts getting in return?	How many of you have seen kelp? Have you been swimming in it?
Does anyone know what *sparingly* means?	What are your feelings about the events that just happened?
How many miles is that?	What connections can you make between your life experiences and those of Karana?
Who are the Aleuts?	What actions would you take toward Captain Mitriff and his crew?
	In what ways are Captain Orlov's and the Aleut hunters' actions similar to other groups of people of today?

Reflection Point 3.4

1. In what ways do the ideas presented in this chapter complement or challenge your present belief system on how students construct meaning?

2. What insights did you gain by observing how your students responded to the instructional strategy you provided?

3. How will you explain to parents and interested others the importance of making explicit intentions and purposes for various literacy events?

Chapter 4

Acknowledging Social Position: When Children Use Evaluative Criteria to Select Partners

Tommy, a third grader, sits at one of the computers in the back of the room. He is using a word processing software program to type and a paint-and-draw program to create illustrations for his published story. Tommy's best friend, Simon, sits next to him, also publishing his adventure story:

Simon: *Tommy, what's your story about?*

Tommy: *Well, it is called "The Magic Jungle," and Keith and his father go into the magic jungle, and it gets dark. The trees block the entrance and then they start hearing noises. There is a roar of a lion and then they bumped into a wishing tree. So they wish for a wishing well... Transform into a lion and kills the octopus. Then it [lion] turns into a human monkey [that] looks like Godzilla and kicks him [Keith] and he is dead. The father is still in the jungle....*

Simon: *Cool. My story is about a spaceship going into outer space.*

Tommy: *Wow! That sounds neat. Let me see your pictures. What's your title?*

Simon: *I haven't decided yet.*

Tommy: *Oh. Let me know. What about "Space Adventure"? Like Space Jam!*

Simon: *I don't know. When I finish it I'll tell you.*

At this point Simon shows Tommy the pictures he has created with the paint-and-draw computer program. His pictures depict a spaceship in outer space, and one picture illustrates what the spaceship looks like on the inside. Tommy follows Simon's lead and shares his own illustrations. The first one is a picture of a tree with a black background. He explains to Simon that this is the magic jungle in which Keith and his father get lost. While these two students share stories and illustrations, they also construct joint meanings of text, as exemplified in Tommy's suggested title for Simon's story.

In Jane's classroom, Michelle and Elaine work on a skill activity sheet for Chapter Three of Island of the Blue Dolphins. When presented with the option of working in pairs, Elaine quickly selected Michelle as her partner. Michelle was quite happy to accept Elaine's offer. The two girls move to a corner in the classroom and begin reading Chapter Three, taking turns reading aloud. The content of the chapter focuses on Karana and her tribe watching Captain Orlov and his crew as they began to slaughter the sea otters. The two girls stop often during the oral reading to clarify ideas or to answer one of the questions on the activity sheet. After reading the first two pages of the chapter, this interchange occurs:

Michelle: So what they are saying is that Ulupe is watching the Aleut woman, and she is bringing news about her and all the other Aleuts and stuff. And then Ramo, Ulupe she said that earlier that, um…

Elaine: Ulupe said that?

Michelle: Said that there was an Aleut woman but nobody believed her because they didn't think they would bring a girl, but now she says that the Aleut girl, the Aleut girl spent a whole afternoon cleaning her skill aprons.

Elaine: Which she never did before.

Michelle: Yeah, while she had been there. And then Ramo—was that earlier in the story? He said that, um, each morning Captain Orlov will sit on a rock besides his tent and comb his beard to make it look as shiny as the Cormorant wings.

*The girls work together, responding to each other and negotiating
ideas about what two of the characters, Ulupe and Ramo, had observed
in watching the Aleut camp. Michelle's response begins with what the
text had said. Elaine adds to Michelle's interpretation by saying that the
Aleut woman had never before cleaned her aprons. As Michelle and
Elaine engage in the literacy event, they appropriate each other's ideas
and those of the text to construct shared understandings.*

In both vignettes, the socially mediated context contributed to children's notions of what it means to engage with text as readers, writers, and meaning makers. The teachers established and orchestrated various groupings for children to read, write, and learn. These groups often have immense influence on the learning process. Student perceptions and social positions impact and sustain motivation to engage in literacy events. Choosing partners, the joint action of the partners, and the dialogue between partners all contribute to the meaning-construction process.

The element of interaction, as limited or extensive as it may be, plays a major role in the meaning-making process. Jerome Bruner (1966), one of the principal architects of the cognitive revolution, once noted that

> [Social interaction] is the basis of human society, this response through reciprocity to other members of one's species, where joint action is needed, where reciprocity is required for the group to attain an objective, then there seem to be processes that carry the individual along into learning, sweep him into a competence that is required in the setting of the group. (p. 125)

To build a frame of reference for discussing social positioning, consider the "social worlds" (Dyson, 1993) teachers and students create in the classroom. As Lerissa explained to Mary, "I really like working with my friends, like writing stories or reading *Nancy Drew* books then talking about them. My friends help me learn and encourage me to ask lots of questions and find out the answers." This sentiment is also exemplified in the fourth-grade classroom. Elaine consistently sought out peer interaction and assistance. Elaine's and Lerrisa's desire to work with peers during literacy events reflects the power of learning in a socially situated context. Following this discussion, we shift to expanding on what social positioning means and how it differs from social status.

We describe how third- and fourth-grade students used evaluative criteria to determine a peer's social position. These criteria influenced the viability of becoming a partner, the motivation to engage in the event, stance toward the literacy event, and, eventually, student responses. The requirements of the event (such as reading, writing stories, group discussion) highlighted the qualities a student needed to be considered a desirable partner. We also illustrate how the operative factors of negotiations, friendships, and chapter books played a major role in shaping social position, motivating students to engage in an event and increasing the will to learn within these two classrooms. Tensions arose when teachers and students were not aware of how influential the evaluative criteria were on social positioning. After closely examining social positioning, we offer strategies that may assist you in discovering and using your own students' criteria for engaging in the meaning-making process.

As we consider the social nature of learning in this chapter, it is important to recognize the varying degrees of social behavior in the classrooms. Tommy and Simon consulted each other for ideas and feedback in the opening vignette, as did Michelle and Elaine. In other instances, the notion of "social" is expanded as a small group of students constructs a shared response or interpretation. The range of social behavior exhibited on any given day in the classroom merely reflects how embedded the social worlds are in the classrooms.

Reflection Point 4.1 _____

Reflect on what you have noticed about the "social" qualities of your students.

1. Do any of your students stand out in a particular way?

2. How might you best respond to and highlight these qualities in your students?

The Importance of the Social World

The social worlds established in the classroom include the official community of the school, the enacted curriculum, and the interactions with the teacher and/or other adults in the classroom (Dyson, 1993). Children participate in the social world around them through verbal and nonverbal actions. As noted earlier, they develop literacy knowledge and behaviors through different interactions with peers and adults. Perhaps John Dewey said it best when he stated,

> About interaction...nature is forever changing and this dynamism results from an unending process of interaction. Things act and react upon one another, and in so doing are reciprocally transformed. This interactive relationship between things constitutes a bond of unity, which contradicts any absolute separation or isolation imposed by dualistic categories.... The quality of experience is a consequence of the character of the interactions, which have occurred. (Dewey, in Archambault, 1966, p. 42)

The words of Dewey suggest that the nature of interaction plays a determining role in the quality of one's experiences, and by extension, on one's learning. The negotiated and jointly constructed understandings of an idea or concept in a literature discussion or conversation exemplify how "things [ideas and language] act and react upon one another, and in so doing are reciprocally transformed" (Dewey, in Archambault, 1966, p. 42). As an illustration of the reciprocal relationship, consider Sammy's comment to Mary:

> I think I influence my friends and help them learn more, like starting to read about big cats, 'cause I saw this show on cheetahs. There's this show I really like called "Cat's Creatures" and it's about wild animals, and so I saw it. One of them was on cheetahs and I started really liking them, and then at the library, I started checking out books on them. And then Lerissa, and my friends started to check out books on cheetahs, and then they started checking out books on big cats in general. Lions and tigers and leopards and stuff like that. Then we would all talk about the cats and cheetahs and stuff at lunch and recess. Now we all want to learn more about lions and leopards.

Both Lerissa and Sammy provide us with some insight into why they enjoy the social interaction with their friends as they participate in the learning process. It is more than sharing ideas; it is sharing experiences.

The opening vignette in Chapter 1 (in which four girls are discussing the book *The Courage of Sarah Noble* and their love of reading) exemplifies what Anne Dyson (1989, 1993) refers to as the "unofficial peer world." These girls participated in their own literacy club, which had all the elements of a "club"—membership, status, and responsibility to engage. When students from different backgrounds and different age groups work together, they each bring to the activity another set of "tools" (such as experiences, knowledge, strategies, and materials) that can be used to construct and negotiate meaning. All members of the group contribute to the construction of meaning and reconceptualize their own ideas, which are then turned into written stories, poems, or plays.

Children move between two worlds, learning how to negotiate and construct meaning within the official world of the classroom and the unofficial world of peers. In many classrooms, Lynn's included, technology may be viewed as a bridge between the official and unofficial worlds. Students access technological tools in a variety of ways, supporting both the official and unofficial worlds. For instance, in the opening vignette of this chapter, Tommy and Simon's writing experience was enhanced by the use of word processing and a paint-and-draw graphics program. They composed and illustrated their stories, all the while interacting with each other.

Students also learn how to position themselves within specific events in which the context of the activity is equally as important as the activity itself. Children try to make sense and construct meaning through negotiations with others in various contexts, which helps them to reconsider and revise their ideas to formulate new knowledge and understandings. As we continued to look closely in these two classrooms, we wondered how the hidden influence of social positioning was played out. Why did children position themselves in particular ways, and what effect did their positioning have on constructing understandings of texts, tasks, and of each other? We need to remind ourselves that reading and writing are socially mediated processes; therefore, we should focus on the process and actions. Before moving on, take a moment to reflect on the ways in which your students interact with each other.

*Reflection Point 4.2*_____

1. What opportunities are provided for your students to socially interact and engage with peers?

2. In what ways are the official and unofficial worlds intersecting in your classroom community?

_____

The Hidden Influence of Social Positioning

Our definition of social positioning is not synonymous with social status or popularity. Rather it is how students use evaluative criteria to decide how they want to position themselves within events, how they want to act and interact with others, and the ways they are positioned by others during interactions (Dillon, 2000; Gee, 1990). In the middle elementary grades, children's decisions about who can and cannot be accepted into the social world plays a significant role in the discourse community.

Although not synonymous, the terms *social positioning* and *social status* have some overlaps. According to Berndt (1983a), the social status of children can include five factors: (1) social behavior, (2) degree of involvement with peers, (3) approach to joining a social group, (4) stability of social groups within the environment, and (5) facility with social skills that enables one to behave appropriately. In her study on helping interactions during literacy events in a third-grade classroom, Jane West (1996) describes how students' interactions and access to help were influenced by their status (Garnica, 1981). She discovered that peers can be a vital source of a wide range of help with literacy learning. She also learned that social status has tremendous influence on children's access to peer help, outweighing other factors such as the type of requests (e.g., for help or for the answer). We have seen some traces of this phenomenon in the classrooms we observed. For example, in the third-grade classroom, William chose Lerissa as a partner for partner reading because he thought Lerissa knew how to behave appropriately and would get the work done on time, so they could earn points for free-choice time. In this example, we see how status played a role in the selection process. However, for the purposes of this discussion, we will focus more on the "positioning" of students as opposed to the status of students.

A student's social position is best described as how peers perceive him or her as a member of the class and as a viable partner for literacy events. Because this perception is based on how a student participates in a particular literacy event, and because it varies across events, social position is a dynamic, fluid notion, not a permanent label. Students' social positions are determined by character traits such as friendliness and willingness to help others, academic performance, behavior, and friendship circles. These positions are influenced when students connect with each other through common interests, including sports, pop culture, and games. Much of these criteria are not explicit or apparent to casual observation. Thus, we consider social positioning to be a hidden influence within the meaning-making process.

Student perceptions of social position are comprised of two essential components: evaluative criteria and access to events. The evaluative criteria children use determines social position within the classroom community, which in turn determines how they are able to access the event. Access to such events includes assisting, collaborating, encouraging, recommending, competing, and distracting.

Constructing Evaluative Criteria

The ways in which children participate and interact with texts, tasks, and each other often indicate social positioning. Some of the literacy events in the two classrooms we observed (such as creative writing, computer time, partner reading, illustrating brochures) allowed for playfulness and talking. None of the events permitted children to fool around on the rug, run or jump in the classroom, aggravate other students, or talk while another person was speaking. Based on these established "rules" for literacy events, the children began to evaluate academic performance and behavior with such descriptors as "smart," "cool," "annoying," "boring," "talkative," or "helpful." The children had specific reasons for evaluating a classmate as they did (see Box 4.1 on page 76).

The students' social positions, then, were determined by their participation in literacy events, which influenced future engagements in events with a chosen partner. The evaluative descriptors change for different events depending on how peers evaluated him or her as a desirable partner for a particular literacy event. Although there was no ranking of social status (i.e., high or low), some of the criteria used in evaluating a peer's social position seemed to imply positive or negative qualities. In the third-grade partner reading event described next, we can see how a student's social position and access to the event influenced how meaning was co-constructed.

Lynn's students participated in daily partner reading as part of the reading/language arts block of time. When it was time to partner read, Lynn called on a student and asked him or her to select a peer. She needed to approve the choice of partners. If there was a questionable selection of partners, Lynn asked, "Do you think that this person is a good choice for you? Do you think you can work with this person to accomplish your goal?" If the answer to either of these questions was "no," then she vetoed the partner choice. Oftentimes students chose the same partner. Lerissa explained why she chose Sammy as a partner to read on this day. "Me and Sammy really, really want to work together when we grow up and be marine biologists and then work at Sea World or something and Marine World and working with the animals. Sammy is really smart." Once partners were chosen and approved by the teacher, the children dispersed around the classroom to read. They sat on the couch, at the back table, on the rug in the front of the room, or at their desks.

On one occasion, Lerissa and Sammy went to the back of the room and moved their chairs close to the counter where Vanilla Bean's cage was located (Vanilla Bean was the class rat that they adored). They were reading *More Stories Julian Tells* (Cameron, 1989), a collection of short stories about such topics as jealousy, loyalty, honesty, friendship, and sibling love. The characters include an 8-year-old African American boy named Julian; his little brother, Huey; and his best friend, Gloria. The girls decided that Sammy would read first, and Sammy counted out the number of pages in the chapter. Meanwhile, Lerissa quickly thumbed through the chapter to see which pages had pictures. Because there were 12 pages to read and almost 4 of the pages had pictures, it worked out evenly that each

---

Box 4.1
Students' Evaluative Criteria and Rationale for Selecting Partners

Criteria:

Smart—knowing a lot of information

Cool—popular among peers

Annoying—not paying attention to the task

Boring—quiet; nonparticipatory

Talkative—talking too much

Bossy—controlling and not respecting equal roles

Helpful—assisted with spelling and encouraged partners to read and write

Students' reasons for terms assigned to classmates:

Rodney liked to share his pictures with Jennifer, explaining, "She is like a really good drawer so I ask her to see her pictures and she says okay, so I show her mine, um...she's cool."

Sammy mentioned in her interview that she liked to work with Lerissa for many reasons. "We talk about stuff we like, like books and animals, and she is smart. We are writing this funny story, 'The Mystery of the Roller Skating Vampire,' and we laugh about it. And when we grow up we want to work with animals. Lerissa is so cool and she has neat ideas. She likes to talk a lot, too."

Jennifer said, "I have only read a few chapter books, but I know Anneka likes to read lots of them. She is so smart."

Elaine stated, "Michelle is a smart and cool partner to work with. She has good ideas."

Rodney mentioned that Tommy was a smart and cool partner as well. "When I had the opportunity to write a Halloween story with someone, I chose Tommy. He usually has some neat ideas."

Jennifer explained in a conversation about reading aloud, "It's hard, I am trying to pay attention when someone is blabbing." And about partner reading, she mentioned, "Sometimes this person can get on my nerves. They might be blabbing when I am trying to tell them about the story." Jennifer further explained, "Rodney is annoying so I don't like to partner read with him. He drives me crazy sometimes."

Kelly's comments regarding Elizabeth included, "I don't like working with her. She doesn't know how to work together. She is kind of bossy about her ideas."

Lerissa exclaimed, "I just don't like to work with him, he is so boring and we never get anything done. I am the one who has to come up with ideas and all the answers."

Clark commented in general about his peers, "They work too slow. I don't want to wait for them."

would read the equivalent of 4 full pages. The title of this chapter was "A Day When Frogs Wear Shoes." After reading the first few pages, Sammy and Lerissa discussed the beginning part of the story when Julian, Gloria, and Huey were afraid to tell Julian's father they were bored:

Sammy: I wonder why Julian's father doesn't like people to be bored?

Lerissa: Probably because then they drive him crazy.

Sammy: Yeah, like sometimes when I am at home and I get bored, I drive my mom crazy.

Lerissa: Yeah, me and my brother do that to our dad, like on the weekends or something.

As they continued to read, Sammy stumbled on the word *scorching*. Lerissa assisted her in sounding out the word.

Sammy: It was "socorching" hot.

Lerissa: I think it is "sc"—like "scor-ching."

Sammy: Yeah, I think you are right, okay, "It was scorching hot."

Lerissa: Does that mean really, really hot?

Sammy: Yeah, I think so, like when a fire is scorching.

Lerissa: Oh, yeah. Okay, keep reading.

After finishing the story, they discussed what they liked to do on a hot summer day.

Sammy: I love to go swimming when it is really hot out.

Lerissa: Yeah, me too, and I like to go and get ice cream.

Sammy: Oh, yeah, me too, and you know my little brother loves ice cream too, but he gets it all over himself; he's only 2.

Lerissa: I used to get it all over myself when I was little but now I am pretty careful.

Sammy: Where is your favorite place to go swimming?

Lerissa: I love to go to the beach, but I only go with my mother. My father takes us to the pool.

Sammy: I like to go swimming in a lake, like when we go camping.

Lerissa: Oh, yeah, that's fun too.

Lerissa assisted Sammy in sounding out the word and discussing the meaning. Because neither student was completely sure, they decided to access background knowledge and negotiate a definition as they read. Lerissa also encouraged Sammy to continue to read. After they finished the story, they discussed what they liked to do on a hot summer day. Both girls had a positive experience and evaluated each other as desirable partners for the partner reading event.

In this example, Lerissa chose Sammy as a partner because of friendship and common interests. Lerissa gained access to the event by asking Sammy to be her partner, and with Sammy's acceptance they engaged in the literacy event together. Typically, the way to gain access into the event was to either choose a partner or to be chosen as a partner. Therefore, the issue of "partner choosing" is directly related to perceptions of a student's social position and is a significant component of meaning making.

Partner reading also occurred for book club participants in Jane and Kathy's classroom. When reading the self-selected literature, the students were able to group themselves according to their own interests and friendships. On most days, one would find Elaine, Kelly, and Marcy partnered up to share in the reading of the chapter. Robert and Michelle occasionally joined together. Clark and Elizabeth, however, were generally observed reading alone, or in Elizabeth's case, with Amy. These two students did not have the positive experiences working with peers that students like Sammy and Lerissa did. In an interview, Clark commented that he did not like to work with others because "they work too slow." For Clark, it was important to complete the task or assignment in the most expeditious way. He did not find value in interacting with his peers. Because he generally completed his work and had interesting comments, Clark was positioned as someone who was "cool," but not accessible to work with.

Elizabeth was the one student in the group who struggled in her interactions with peers and with the teachers. Similar to Clark, she was a competent reader, but this did not seem to matter to the other students. During book club reading, Elizabeth often asked Amy to read with her because the other students did not accept her into their groups. They had positioned Elizabeth as an undesirable partner. One morning, however, Kelly and Elizabeth decided to try working together on comprehension questions for a chapter from *Island of the Blue Dolphins*. As the activity started, Kelly and Elizabeth struggled to construct a meaningfully nego-tiated response:

Kelly: It has to be more than a dozen [referring to a question]. Elizabeth, you are supposed to be working in partners, not alone.

Elizabeth: I know. I'm trying to.

Kelly: You are already on number six and I didn't get number four or five. I'm sitting here and you are just writing, and I don't know what you are writing down.

Elizabeth: I'm trying to.

Kelly: We're supposed to work in partners. Do you know what that is? Partners is [are] two people working together, not alone.

In this exchange, there was disagreement on how to answer the question. Kelly's frustration when working with Elizabeth to answer some compre-hension questions resulted in both girls completing the task individually.

Students' social positions also influenced access to events. If a stu-dent was considered to be helpful, he or she was more apt to be chosen as a partner, as opposed to a student who was considered to be annoying or bossy. Likewise, students were not likely to initiate discussions with partners who were too talkative, as the extraneous talking might inter-fere with the completion of an assignment or cause them to lose minutes for free choice time.

There are different ways children gain access to an event within the social structure of the classroom. (Box 4.2 on page 80 provides an expla-nation of the ways students enter into events.) Once students become involved in the event, their ways of participating are related to the purpose of the event itself. What children bring to an event, specifically back-ground knowledge and experiences, and what they encounter in the event affects the nature of the interaction and the evaluative criteria that guided them through meaning-making opportunities.

The social positioning of individuals within the group affects students within the learning community. Bloome and Bailey (1992) suggest that participants continuously negotiate identities and social relationships during events and that these negotiations depend on one's ability to

---

Box 4.2
Gaining Access to Events

Choosing a partner:
The student was allowed to choose a partner to work with.

Chosen as a partner:
Another student chose the focal student as a partner.

Volunteer:
A student could volunteer to participate in the event.

Initiate discussion:
A student could initiate a discussion with another student or in the whole class group.

---

participate in the event and other related events. The social relationships constitute speaking rights and obligations, authority for interpretation, rights to tell or retell stories, and access to material resources. In addition, relationships and positions carried within the classroom context can influence the ways in which learners demonstrate knowledge.

Reflection Point 4.3

Observe three to five students as they participate in socially mediated events.

1. How do your students evaluate each other's position in the event and gain access into various literacy events?

2. Who selects whom?

3. What might be the criteria they are using to make their decisions?

Instructional Strategies Used to Discover How Students Evaluate and Perceive Peers as Partners

There are a number of instructional strategies designed to better understand the influential nature of social positioning. These strategies and activities also work well for assessment purposes, as you aim to recognize how powerful students' own interests and desires to work with particular peers influence the meaning-construction process. Additionally, we can glean information about how students benefit from exposure to responses from peers with different perspectives.

Photo-Sorting Activity

Developed by Harris (1979, 1989), the photo-sorting activity is one way to uncover how students perceive various literacy events, tasks, and the value of working with peers. By using photographs, students reflect on their impressions and perceptions of the event, rather than the event itself. The constructs may be modified to best meet students' needs or to be used as an assessment tool. Following is a description of how to implement the activity:

1. Take photographs of reading and writing situations observed in your own classroom, such as
   - partner reading: two children reading a book together
   - free choice time: three or four children playing a reading game on the rug
   - journal writing: children writing in their journal at their desks
   - creative writing: child writing a story alone or collaboratively with others
   - read-aloud: the teacher reading aloud to the whole class or a small group
   - group read-aloud: each child in the group reads aloud a paragraph
   - computer time: child working on the computer
   - independent reading: children reading a book alone
   - group discussion: small-group or whole-class discussion
   - teacher-led discussion: teacher guiding the discussion

2. Present each child with a photo. Discuss the photograph to ensure common understanding of the activity.

3. Ask each child to sort the photos four times according to one of the following pairs of constructs:
   • activities I like to do (+)/ activities I don't like to do (-)
   • activities I find easy to do (+)/ activities I find difficult to do (-)
   • activities that motivate me to read (+)/ activities that don't moti-vate me to read (-)
   • conditions (physical environment, people, titles of books) that make me want to read and write (+)/ conditions (physical envi-ronment, people, titles of books) that take away from my want-ing to read and write (-)

4. Following each sort, ask the child for the reasons he or she chose that photo to answer the construct. Fill in the grid with the child's answers. The sorting activity reveals what each child associates with particular literacy events and/or activities and how ongoing partic-ipation in such tasks shapes his or her constructs of learning, in general, and more specifically, reading and writing.

Figure 8 presents an example of a photo-sorting grid completed for Jen-nifer in Lynn's third-grade classroom.

Reader/Writer Interest Inventory

To find out more about your students' reading and writing interests, you can either interview them or create an inventory for them to fill in (Riordan-Karlsson, 1997). Figure 9 (see page 85) provides an example of a reader/writer inventory. Asking the four categories of questions can provide some insight into your students' worlds and their perceptions of themselves as readers and writers. You can also learn about their participatory preferences, such as which activities they prefer to do alone or with others.

Circle Writing

Circle writing encourages students to formulate responses and chal-lenge one another using written language. This activity provides an op-portunity for students to respond at their own individual level and benefit

Figure 8
Jennifer's Photo-Sorting Activity

Construct Situation	Activities I like to do (+)/ Activities I don't like to do (–)	Activities I find easy to do (+)/ Activities I find difficult to do (–)	Activities that motivate me to read (+)/ Activities that don't motivate me to read (–)	Conditions that make me want to read and write (+)/ Conditions that take away from wanting to read and write (–)
Partner Reading	–Sometimes this person can get on my nerves; they might be blabbing when I am trying to tell them about the story.		+When my partner helps me with words or I help her.	
Free Choice Time			+A couple of my friends like reading too. Anneka is very smart so I know it's a good book.	+When we earn minutes so I can play on the computer.
Journal Writing	+It's fun and you can learn stuff.		+Writing is really fun: I just like writing.	
Creative Writing	+I love drawing and coloring things. I like talking with friends and deciding on stories.	+It's easy and fun to decide what to do.		
Read-Aloud	–It's hard, I am trying to pay attention when someone is blabbing.		+It's pretty fun to listen to the teacher and she reads good books.	+It gets me interested to read good books.

(continued)

Figure 8 (continued)				
Jennifer's Photo-Sorting Activity				
Group Read-Aloud	+I pretty much like that cause it's pretty fun.		+Reading interests me a lot—so we can read aloud with other students.	
Computer Time	+Computers are really fun. I like typing stories.	+I learn how to do neat things and it's easy to find the key.	+I just love to work on the computer—it's one of my favorite things in the whole world.	+Like I told you, I love reading books and I love typing on the computer.
Independent Reading	+I like reading because it interests me into writing books.	+I think the book Sammy is reading would be pretty neat.		
Group	–You have to get picked on and sometimes I don't have anything to say.		–You have to get picked and I don't really have anything to say.	+When we get to talk about the books we are reading.
Teacher-led Discussion			–You have to get picked and I don't really have anything to say.	

from exposure to responses from peers with different perspectives. In small groups of three, students respond to an open-ended question formulated by the teacher or by the entire class. Each student has the opportunity to respond through agreement, disagreement, elaboration, or illustration. By sharing responses, students position themselves within the event using writing as a tool.

To illustrate this strategy, we use *just [sic] Juice* (Hesse, 1998) to show how students may express their ideas and understandings about a significant theme or aspect of the story. The strategy is outlined in Figure 10 on page 86.

Figure 9
Reader/Writer Interest Inventory

Personal questions:

Do you like to read/write?

What do you like to read/write?

Do you remember when you learned how to read?

What have been some of your past experiences with reading/writing?

Did you always like/dislike it? Why?

How would you describe yourself as a reader/writer?

Motivation (affective) questions:

Do you like to learn new things?

What motivates you to learn?

Why do you want to learn some things and not others?

What makes something interesting to learn?

Are you influenced by what your friends like to do in school?

Do you talk with your friends about good books you have read?

Do your parents suggest good books to read?

What are your favorite kinds of books to read?

What do you read at home?

What recreational activities do you like to do in school during free time?

What recreational activities do you like to do at home?

Social questions:

Do you like to work with others or alone?

What do you like most about your classroom?

What do you like least about your classroom?

What is your favorite activity that you do with your friends in class?

Cognitive questions:

How do you think you learn new knowledge?

How do you know if you understand something you have read?

How do you make meaning?

Do you ever negotiate with a friend as to what something means?

What do you do if you don't understand something you have just read?

From Riordan-Karlsson, M. (1997). *Negotiations, friendships, and chapter books: The influence of meaning authority, peer interaction, and student perceptions on reader motivation and meaning construction in a third grade classroom.* Unpublished dissertation, University of California, Berkeley, CA.

Figure 10
Circle Writing Strategy

- After reading the story, have students form groups of three and hand them a couple of index cards.

- Ask one student in the group to respond to the question, "Juice and her family are struggling to keep the house. How does Pa's difficulty reading affect the family?"

- After a few minutes, have students pass their card clockwise.

- The second student in the group agrees, disagrees, or elaborates in writing or through illustrations.

- The third student adds to the previous comments and constructs a new question or statement. The other two group members respond.

Reflection Point 4.4

Administer one of the strategies shared in the latter portion of this chapter.

1. What new information was gained by discovering how your students perceive others as viable partners?

2. How did you use the information?

The hidden influence of social positioning determines, in many cases, the ways in which children interact and work with each other in socially mediated settings. It is important to further investigate the choices students make when working with partners in order to better understand how they position themselves and evaluate each other in the classroom. Now that we have explored two of the three influences, we will move into a discussion on the role of interpretive authority and alternative sources of meaning. In the next chapter, we ask the questions, "Whose responses are perceived as contributing to the meaning-making process?" and "Who has the authority to determine what is an acceptable answer?"

Valuing the Response:
Examining Alternative Sources of
Meaning and Interpretive Authority

*The book club group decides one day to ask each other questions
about the story they are reading,* The Mouse and the Motorcycle.
*Amy talks with them for a few minutes about the types of questions that
they might want to consider and the difference between literal, known-
answer questions and interpretive, applicative questions that require
more critical thinking. After this explanation, the students write their
questions and share them with the group. Clark initiates the discussion:*

Clark: *Why does Ralph like the motorcycle?*

Kelly: *Why does he like it?*

Jake: *'Cause it works.*

Kelly: *Why did he like the motorcycle? Because he can ride it.*

Clark: *Okay. Jake's turn.*

Jake: *What does Ralph do when he was being sucked in by the
           vacuum cleaner?*

Michelle: *He holds onto the motorcycle.*

Clark: *Cool, okay, that's nice. Robert's turn.*

Robert: *No.*

Clark: *Robert.*

Kelly: *Why was Keith friendly to Ralph?*

Clark: *Because he was a mouse and Keith likes mice.*

Elizabeth: *And he could talk. Ralph could talk and it was the first talking mouse he heard.*

Clark: *No.*

Elizabeth: *Yeah.*

Robert: *Does anybody think that maybe he likes Ralph?*

Clark positions himself in this conversation as having authority. He quickly initiates the discussion, determines who will speak, and evaluates others' responses. The conversation continues.

Robert: *Does anybody know what it means when they say, "I will give you the keys to my heart?"*

Elizabeth: *That question is hard.*

Elaine: *I know…*

Marcy: *The keys to your heart...*

Elaine: *Love him and love him forever.*

Clark: *I know what that means. I know what that means. That means you can unlock the door and make a quick get-away.*

Amy: *Do you remember when she was singing it?*

Clark: *I know she was singing it in that old song.*

Kelly: *Why don't we start over?*

Clark: *Why does Ralph like the motorcycle?*

Kelly: *Because he is tired of walking all over the hotel.*

Clark: *BZZZZZ [buzzer sound]*

Amy: *What is wrong with that answer, Clark?*

Clark: *How can he walk all the way around the hotel?*

Kelly: *Well, not around it. He's getting tired of walking.*

In this conversation, Clark assumes a powerful role in the conversation by stating that he knows the answer to Robert's question. Kelly suggests starting over, to which Clark quickly restates his question, and when a response is shared, he evaluates it as inaccurate. Others in the conversation attempt to participate by responding with possible interpretations, and Kelly tries to clarify her response to more closely match Clark's expectation.

In Lynn's third-grade class, Jennifer and Rodney are writing entries in their respective journals after completing the last chapter in The Courage of Sarah Noble. They partner read the chapter, then sit at their desks, which are in the same group, and begin writing their journal entries.

Jennifer: Hey Rodney, have you ever had to use courage like Sarah?

Rodney: Yeah, when I went to camp and they told me there were wolves—so I stayed up all night. Then when there were no wolves I could sleep the next night.

Jennifer: Have you ever been somewhere and met people that did not look like you or spoke another language? Was it scary?

Rodney: Yeah, I have been other places where they didn't speak....

Jennifer: Me too. I was scared. What do you think was the most important lesson Sarah learned?

Rodney: To keep up her courage and not to be afraid. Also she taught the Indian children some things and she learned new games from them.

Jennifer: That was neat. I remember I missed my mom when I went to visit my cousins for a week—the only time in my whole life and I was sad but not afraid.

Rodney: Did you like the story?

Jennifer: Yeah, how 'bout you?

Rodney: Yes, because it reminded me of when I went to camp and was scared. That's what I am writing about right now.

Jennifer: I am writing about being courageous; how do you think you spell that?

Rodney: Like courage and then add o-u-s.

Jennifer: Okay, thanks, then I'm also gonna write what Sarah and her brother and sisters talked about when they saw each other after a long time.

Rodney: Let me see your pictures.

Jennifer: Sure, but wait until I'm done. Then I'll show you all
of them.

*As these two talk and write, they weave together ideas from the
story and from personal experiences. The task at hand has supported a
predominantly aesthetic stance. The resulting journal entry from Jennifer
reflects the comments shared in their discussion.*

Chapter Eleven—My Family!

I was so happy to see my mom today it has ben [been] so long since
I last seen her. My mom was shocked to see that I was wearing moccasins!
And she askd [asked] me where my dress was. I told her it was hanging
in my room and that my cloths are too heavy to wear when I am playing
my games. I told my mom I was courageous like she told me. I was happy to see my little sister and my brother and I told him the Indians were
my friends and they will be friends with him too.

*Both Rodney and Jennifer have much to contribute in this writing
event. They are able to relate to Sarah's fear of the unknown and sympa-
thize with her longing for her mother and siblings. Rodney and Jennifer
view Sarah through their own personal experiences. In doing so, they are
able to demonstrate authority and ownership of ideas.*

We share these moments in the classroom to illustrate the notion
of interpretive authority. As you read the vignette about Clark,
what was your first impression? Did Clark seem as though he
overran the group, or did it seem as though the others appreciated his
"take charge" viewpoint? How did you feel about his willingness to evaluate his peers' responses? In the creative writing event, Jennifer and Rodney worked well together, sharing ideas and possibilities. Did the
authority seem balanced between them?

In this chapter, we examine the notion of interpretive authority, a hidden influence on meaning making. Similar to stance and social positioning,
interpretive authority is a fluid entity, dependent on texts, tasks, participants, and context. The ways in which interpretations are shared in the
learning community and levels of engagement are displayed among the

participants indicate how interpretive authority may be played out. Tensions arise surrounding interpretive authority and meaning making when participants are not able to engage in the event as knowledgeable contributors.

What Is Interpretive Authority?

The daily literature conversations and events among students and teachers in the two classrooms reveal that authority within events is discernable in a number of ways. Interpretive authority involves who is speaking, what the speaker is saying (the content), and how other group members receive the response. To better understand interpretive authority, we considered where teachers and students located meaning during a literacy event—whether it was within the reader's own experiences, information from the text, or knowledge from outside sources. Location of meaning for a text is influenced by teachers' and students' beliefs about literacy and learning, and it determines the content of the interpretation, or the *what* that is said. Moreover, the links and connections readers make to outside references, known as *intertextual links*, play a role in where meaning is located.

In addition to knowing where meaning is located, we considered the types of roles participants assumed during literacy events, including writing time. When teachers and students interact with each other, they assume discourse roles that influence the ways in which interpretations of text and ideas are made public and subsequently, levels of participation are shared. These roles involve knowing how to challenge, accept, confirm, evaluate, and resist others' points of view. The various roles depend on participants' perceptions of the event and other group members.

Interpretive authority takes into consideration location of meaning, including the use of intertextual links and discourse roles. Those with interpretive authority have their interpretations acknowledged and validated by others in the group, and they determine the validity and viability of another's response. Clark's participation in the opening vignette exemplifies how he garnered and utilized his interpretive authority. He was the first to initiate the discussion and share his question, he evaluated responses, and he directed others to participate. The hidden influence of interpretive authority shapes how teachers and students respond to texts, tasks, and each other.

Reflection Point 5.1 _____

The opening vignettes demonstrated the diverse ways in which the students negotiate and construct meaning of text.

1. In thinking about your own classroom and students, what are some ways your learners negotiate and construct meaning from text?

2. Are they encouraged to seek answers outside of the text?

3. Are they aware that there are multiple sources of authority other than the text? How do you validate a response in a discussion?

4. How might you encourage your students to value alternative sources of meaning?

Location of Meaning

Location and source of meaning are constructed and mediated through various belief systems about teaching and learning. The ways in which the teachers responded and reacted to students' interpretations of texts suggest that location of meaning significantly influences the direction and outcomes of the discussions and tasks at hand. Where one believes meaning resides contributes to how one *reads* the text (the adopted stance) and to how one responds in a discussion (to ask for clarification, to justify, or to defend) (Flint, 1997).

The interpretations and, ultimately, the meaning-construction process, are reflective of types and locations of meaning. Harris (1989) determined four types of meaning that can occur and should be considered in the meaning-construction process—personal, group, task, and text. Personal meanings are built from a student's background and cultural practices. Students incorporate themselves into the response, such as Marcy's comment regarding the possibility of Ralph and his relatives (the mice) living with Keith (the little boy) in *The Mouse and Motorcycle*: "I would let the whole family come. I wouldn't tell them [Keith's parents]. I would just put them in the cage." Group meanings are built from shared experiences and agendas. This can also be seen in the discussion in Chapter 3 (see page 54) in which the fourth graders negotiated a shared interpretation of the benefits and difficulties of being a mouse.

Task meanings are more process oriented and based on knowing social conventions and expectations in various literacy events. For example, when Kelly and Elizabeth struggled to work together on a partner event, they both conceptualized the task at hand differently, resulting in a breakdown of meaning construction (see Chapter 4, page 79). Finally, text meanings are generated by what the author and illustrator intended for the book, and they are quite easy to locate with conversation starters such as, "What do you think the island looks like? The description is in the book. It is very detailed." Text meanings presume that what is evident in the text is the appropriate and accurate response or interpretation. The location of meaning—whether it is within the student's personal experiences, negotiated among participants, or evident in the text—plays a significant role in how interpretive authority is manifested in literacy events.

Let us examine a creative writing event in the third grade. Claudia and Lerissa collaborated on a story, and although they were quite talkative, they understood that the discussion of ideas and details was an essential component of the creative writing process. The girls chose to write about a girl living in the 1700s. The collaboration invited a great deal of discussion about the plot of the story, which they decided to model after the story they just read, *The Courage of Sarah Noble*. The following is their discussion about the character's name and plot of the story:

Lerissa: What should we name her, the girl in our story?

Claudia: I don't know, how about Elizabeth? That sounds like an old fashioned name.

Lerissa: Maybe. Well where is she going on her journey? And is she going with her father?

Claudia: Yeah, like Sarah did. What about an island like Island of the Blue Dolphins?

Lerissa: That's neat, but we can't send her to the same island.

> Claudia: What about Hawaii?
>
> Lerissa: Yeah, I always wanted to go there.
>
> Claudia: My parents have been there.
>
> Lerissa: Okay, she will go to Hawaii with her father. Let's write that.

The collaborative partnership assisted and encouraged each writer to think of ideas and associations. Claudia recommended Hawaii as a destination, and Lerissa agreed. Connections to other books such as *The Courage of Sarah Noble* and *Island of the Blue Dolphins* were visible. (These are known as intertextual links; the next section of this chapter expands on this idea.) Claudia had recently read *Island of the Blue Dolphins* for Sustained Silent Reading (SSR) time; she therefore made associations between the characters of Sarah and Karana. Themes in both stories included survival and love of family, which were interesting and attractive to the girls. As they wrote their story, they both accessed background knowledge. For instance, Claudia included her personal knowledge when she mentioned that her parents had been to Hawaii. The next day they decided on a name for their character, Cindy Draft, and proceeded to write an entertaining story. The following is an excerpt from their story:

Cindy Draft—A Great Story

Cindy was riding her welsh pony, (Sarah), back to her house. When her father came out with a candle and said, "Cindy, I'm going to a place called Hawaii. I'm going to build a house there. Oh, father can I go? I'll cook for you" said Cindy. "You may," said Tom Draft. "But if you come with [me] Cindy, you have to have a lot of courage." "I will. I will," said Cindy. So Cindy rode Sarah back into the stable. Tomorrow we're leaving for our jernny [journey]. "Your mother knows about the jernny [journey]. But she doesn't know that you're coming. I'll tell your mother tonight." Cindy woek [woke] up the next morning and got ready. Tom Draft told Cindy to get in their carraige [carriage] and get Acorn and Wanda, the family horses. So Cindy did as she was told. They got in the carriage and rode to the mereena [marina] and got a boat. They saled [sailed] for a week. Fineilly [finally] they were there! When they got there they met a Native Hawaiian. Her name was very hard to say so they called her Jackie.

Clearly the authors borrowed ideas from both, *The Courage of Sarah Noble* and *Island of the Blue Dolphins*. They added details that made it apparent that the story was set in the 1700s and incorporated the ideas that the character meets a Native Hawaiian with a difficult name to say. As Claudia and Lerissa collaboratively wrote this story, the source of meaning authority resided within the texts they read, within each other as writers, and in the negotiation between text and writers. The source of meaning authority was not located in only one location, but in multiple locations.

Intertextual Links: Connections to Other Stories and Experiences

Source and location of meaning are also influenced by the connections made among personal experiences, other texts, imagination, and world knowledge. Hartman (1991) notes that intertextuality is an "orchestrated effort to mobilize potential knowledge, which generates interconnections among many knowledge sources, resulting in a web of meaning" (p. 527). The various links students and teachers make contribute to the ways in which interpretations are constructed. When students have opportunities to voice their connections, whether to a personal experience or to a nugget of information learned elsewhere, the responses and understandings of the story are richer and more complex, as evidenced in the creative writing event with Claudia and Lerissa. Intertextual links provide students with a wealth of possible places to connect knowledge and construct meaningful interpretations, thereby strengthening the web of meaning Hartman talks about. Group members in literature discussion groups determine the relevance and relatedness of the intertextual link to the meaning-making process. If a response is deemed irrelevant and not related, the participant contributing the response is viewed with less interpretive authority. Conversely, a person making intertextual links may be perceived as having more interpretive authority because intertextual links may deepen the meaning-making process.

Over the course of the book club event and the literature units, the fourth-grade students shared many intertextual links. Jane and Kathy encouraged their students on a number of occasions to bring in personal experiences and world knowledge to contribute to the meaning-making process (as seen in Chapter 3). Often, these links confirmed ideas and understandings. The connections and links did not always have to be voiced in a discussion. Kathy and Jane assigned a book report for *Otherwise Known as Sheila, the Great* and a travel brochure for *Island of the Blue Dolphins*. These were two writing events in which intertextual links contributed to the meaning-making process, and therefore supported students' interpretive authority.

The travel brochure writing task required students to create travel brochures to highlight the reasons why a traveler might want to visit the island. Jane and Kathy talked quite a bit about what might be on a travel brochure (foods to eat, activities to do, and location), and they showed samples of brochures from a travel agency. Robert and Elaine invested a lot of time on their travel brochures. Interestingly, both of these students struggled with the reading process as defined and constructed in Jane's classroom, but this assignment enabled them to create understandings in a different way.

Robert's travel brochure (see Figure 11) only indicated events and activities one could do while visiting a particular place, and he did not include some of the other ideas proposed by Jane and Kathy. The listed activities were based more on his experiences, rather than what was identified in the text. On the front cover Robert wrote, "Welcome to the Island of the Blue Dolphin." The use of the term *welcome* suggested his knowledge of an appropriate greeting used when inviting someone to visit a particular place. On the inside of the brochure Robert drew pictures on three quarters of the page and on the bottom quarter he wrote, "You can tack [take] a boat ride. You can go site [sight] seeing. You can go swimming with dolphin. You can ride the dolphin. You can play with the dog. You can make them fech [fetch]."

In this activity, Robert demonstrated that he had a clear sense of events to participate in when visiting an island. He appropriated travel discourse by using the term *site seeing*. Robert also incorporated his knowledge about swimming with and riding dolphins, as seen in a local animal park, Marine World. Having dogs "fetch" was a personal experience Robert shared, as this was not an activity described in the text.

On the back side of the brochure, Robert wrote, "Calimb [climb] the pame [palm] theres [trees] and tack [take] cowcanut [coconut]. You can play in the sun." Robert again revealed his personal knowledge of what

Figure 11
Robert's Travel Brochure

Welcome To the island of the blue Dolphin

you can tack a boat ride. you can go site seeing.

you can go swimming with dolphin. you can ride the dolphin.

you can play with the dog. you can make them fach

Calimb the pame there and talk cowkanat you can play in the san.

islands should have in terms of vegetation. There was no mention of palm trees and coconuts when the island's vegetation was described in the story. When designing his travel brochure, Robert clearly located meaning within his own experiences rather than from the text. This enabled him to make intertextual links and connections to other sources. Throughout the brochure, he shared personal and world knowledge to construct an understanding of visiting islands and creating travel brochures.

Elaine's travel brochure also demonstrated connections from her own experiences (see Figure 12). Her cover did not embellish on the visiting or welcoming aspect; it simply said, "Island of the Blue Dolphin." Within the brochure itself, Elaine titled the sections "Activities," "Things to Do," "Food," and " Craft." In each of the sections she listed a number of possibilities: build sand castles, swim in the ocean, play with Rontuaro; go on a cone [canoe] ride, pick flowers, eat food, teach our language; mack [make] a scurt [skirt], mack [make] a hair buret [barrette], mack [make] earrings, mack [make] shoes, mack [make] a shurt [shirt]; and eat octipose [octopus], crabe [crab], clamb [clam], devel [devil] fish, fish.

Elaine's inclusion of building sand castles, playing with Rontuaro (a dog in the story), teaching our language, and the various food selections highlighted that meaning was a negotiation between her experiences and text. Elaine incorporated her personal experiences of playing on the beach and building sand castles, but she also recalled information from the text about the types of things the main character in the story was busy making on the island, with the exception of the hair barrette. This was another example of an intertextual link brought into the meaning-making process.

The travel brochure writing activity provided an opportunity for the students to incorporate intertextual links and connections as they created these documents. The constructed understandings revealed not only where meaning resided for each of the students, but also a sense of authority in what was important to include on the brochure. For Robert and Elaine, two marginalized readers in the classroom, the opportunity to construct interpretations from outside sources and personal experiences contributed to their own interpretive authority and increased their social positioning in the classroom. The travel brochures were displayed on a bulletin board, which enabled others to gain an understanding of Robert's and Elaine's meaning making.

Figure 12
Elaine's Travel Brochure

Discourse Roles

Students' participation in classroom events plays a significant role in how meanings are constructed and negotiated in the socially situated context of the classroom. In any classroom event in which students interact with each other and the teacher, there are a range of discourse roles available to them. Discourse roles involve the intent and structure of the response. When we observed and documented engagement patterns in literature discussions and other events, we were interested in how participants (both students and teachers) entered into the discussion, how they managed to share the "floor," how they contributed relevant ideas and information, and how teachers and students determined the validity of certain responses and interpretations.

The range of discourse roles depends on the purpose established for the discussion. In many of the literacy events orchestrated by Jane and Kathy, the stance toward texts, tasks, and students was one in which remembering information from the text was paramount. In other words, Jane and Kathy assumed a more efferent stance toward literacy events. Given this stance, the teachers monitored students' levels of comprehension. In doing so, the amount of talk was not necessarily evenly distributed. The following excerpt is a conversation that took place early in *Island of the Blue Dolphins*, when the Aleuts and Karana's family first met each other.

Jane:	How do you think they felt? What do you think the trouble was? What do you think the problem was? Who was the bad guy before? Jake, who was the bad guy before?
Jackson:	The Aleuts.
Jane:	No.
Jackson:	The captain?
Jane:	Captain who?
Jackson:	Orlov?
Jane:	No, who was the bad guy before?
Jackson:	Captain Mitriff.
Jane:	Yes, and who said that?
Jackson:	Captain Orlov.
Jane:	Captain Orlov. Why do you think Captain Orlov said Captain Mitriff was a fool? Michelle, why do you think?

[There is no response from Michelle.]

Jane: I'm going to read that paragraph again. I want you to follow along and think about it as I read it. [reads from the chapter] "'You remember another hunt,'" Captain Orlov said when my father was silent. 'I have heard of it too. It was led by Captain Mitriff who was a fool and is now dead. The trouble arose because you and your tribe did all the hunting.' 'We hunted,' said my father, 'but the one you call a fool wished us to hunt from one moon to the next never ceasing.'"

Elaine: I think he was a fool because, ummm, he was in Captain…

Jane: I think you are stumbling. You are thinking, but you are stumbling, Kelly?

Kelly: Because they hunted.

Jane's responsibilities in this discussion included questioning students on their knowledge, determining and orchestrating the order in which students spoke (i.e., calling on various students to respond), and providing evaluative feedback. In this structure of talk, students generally have few opportunities to explore divergent ideas or to challenge a peer's contribution. With the location of meaning residing in the text, the discourse roles available tend to be that of initiator, responder, and evaluator, with the teacher or more knowledgeable peer assuming the more powerful roles of initiator and evaluator. Recall for a moment how Clark assumed a similar pattern of discourse when asked to share questions with peers in the opening vignette.

Recent research on teacher-led and student-led discussions suggests that other patterns of discourse may support a wider range of discourse roles (Almasi, 1996; Barr & Dreban, 1991; McMahon & Raphael, 1997; Wiencek & O'Flahavan, 1994). Understandings culled from Vygotsky (1978) and others (see Bruner, 1986; Cazden, 1986; Ruddell & Unrau, 1994) note that learning is a social endeavor and that by enabling students to share understandings, new ideas are introduced in the literacy event. This pattern of talk does not require one person to respond every other turn, and more divergent interpretations become a valued part of the conversation. Discourse roles are expanded and more participants gain authority within the conversation. As Vogt (1996) states, "The responses, though individual and personal, are clarified, altered, strengthened, and enhanced when shared with others, and variety and approximation rather than correctness are the desired outcomes" (p. 182). In these instances, a greater number of students verbalize more, both in quality and quantity, and it appears that meaning making is enhanced.

Upon reviewing the literature conversations in the two classrooms, we constructed a taxonomy of discourse roles evidenced by these teachers and students (see Box 5.1). These roles exemplified the ways in which the children and teachers responded to texts, tasks, and each other. Of course, in other conversations, with other participants, different roles may exist.

To illustrate the ways in which the discourse roles were enacted, we return to a literature discussion carried out by the book club group in Jane's classroom. The book club selected *Hundred Penny Box* to read as a final book for the group. Recall that *Hundred Penny Box* is a relatively short story about Michael, who tries to understand his Great-Great-Aunt Dew. She is nearing 100 years old and lives with Michael and his parents.

Box 5.1
Various Types of Discourse Roles

- Acceptor/Confirmer: participant accepts and agrees with a response (My favorite part was that too.)
- Catalyst: participant initiates a new or idea or topic of discussion (Motorcycles aren't very comfortable.)
- Challenger: participant challenges an interpretation (Nuh-uh, it doesn't say that. I know, like we never knew that. Duh.)
- Defender: participant justifies or defends his or her own interpretation (I thought I heard his name.)
- Director: participant determines who speaks next (It's Robert's turn.)
- Evaluator: participant evaluates the responses and interpretations (Not exactly, I don't think there are any hay wagons in Chapter Thirteen.)
- Informer: participant shares personal or world-based information (I don't know the ones in English, 'cause I say them in Spanish. I went to CCD in Spanish.)
- Inquisitor: participant questions ideas; wonders (Why is Keith friendly to Ralph?)
- Responder: participant responds to a question asked (The nose is toward the west and the tail toward the east.)

Michael enjoys spending time with Aunt Dew, listening to the many wonderful stories she has to tell. Aunt Dew has an old mahogany box where she keeps pennies, symbolic of keepsakes and memories. As a penny is pulled out of the box a story is told. There are family tensions as Michael's mother tries to take care of Aunt Dew and does not recognize the significance of the box to Aunt Dew's life and stories. The students were about three quarters of the way through the story when this conversation occurred:

Elizabeth:	You know how she has the hundred-penny box? I just figured out she has a dollar.
Robert:	I know, like we never knew that. Duh.
Kelly:	Michael asks Aunt Dew how it feels to be 100 years old.
Robert:	His mom wants her to get rid of the box.
Kelly:	I think she is going to give it to him.
Elizabeth:	We aren't talking about the bear right now [referring to an old bear Michael had as a baby].
Robert:	I thought she was going to give him the box.
Kelly:	She probably did.
Robert:	She [Michael's mother] is bringing up his bear from a long time ago and his friend Corky and then he doesn't need the bear any more.
Elaine:	I know.

The discourse roles the students assumed and made visible within the group expanded from the responder role to that of informer, challenger, confirmer/acceptor, and speculator. The group puzzled over the events that occurred in the story and tried to sort out their confusion about whether or not Aunt Dew was going to give Michael the box. Elizabeth and Robert brought in another aspect of the story—that of Michael holding onto his teddy bear from years ago. The conversation continued, and at one point Amy shared a personal note of interest, "One thing I thought was interesting that Robert and I read today was how Michael's mom was saying that it was okay for Michael to hold onto his teddy bear for as long as he needed it. You know she wasn't going to give it away. It was going to be Michael's decision to give it away, but then…." Kelly quickly picked up on this and stated, "But then throws away all of Aunt Dew's stuff."

Robert challenged, "That's different." Marcy challenged Robert, "It's the same. I think it is the same because Michael got to decide if he wanted it or not. He got to make his own decision and Aunt Dew should too." Amy added, "I think so too. If Michael was allowed to make his decision about the teddy bear…." Kelly jumped in, "Why can't Aunt Dew? If Michael could when he was little, why can't Aunt Dew when she's older?"

The discourse roles in this part of the conversation included more challenges from Robert and Marcy. Kelly was interested in pursuing a line of thinking about how it seemed unfair that Michael can hold onto old treasures, but Aunt Dew is not supposed to.

Reflection Point 5.2

Use a tape recorder to record two different discussions. You should initiate the first discussion as the teacher. The second discussion should be initiated by a group of students.

1. What are some of the differences you notice between the two discussions?

2. What discourse roles do you and your students assume? Recognize that sometimes the roles are not very clear cut, but are implicit in how students respond and participate.

3. Who talks the most? The least?

In Lynn's third-grade class, the children sat in a circle on the reading rug anticipating a group discussion about *The Courage of Sarah Noble*. Group discussion was structured so that a student could only speak if his or her hand was raised and if one was chosen by the previous speaker, thereby encouraging many students to assume the director role. Not raising a hand was an indication that a student did not want to participate at that moment.

Lynn initiated the discussion by saying, "Now that we have all finished reading *The Courage of Sarah Noble*, I would like for each of you to share something about the book that you liked." Daniel was the first one chosen and began the discussion, "I remember when her father wanted to shoot the deer and she said, 'No! Don't shoot it!' I liked how she defended the deer." After he finished, he chose the next person to speak. Claudia always raised her hand, so she was happy to be selected next. "I remember when they were playing a game before her father came back," she said. Lynn prompted Claudia to think a little deeper about her response, asking, "Do you think she was happy or sad?" "She was both happy to see her father, but sad to leave her new friends the Indians," answered Claudia, who then pointed to Velma, who eagerly added, "She was very excited to see her mother." Next, Anneka remarked, "I thought it was cool that she got to wear deerskin clothes and shoes. So she didn't have to wear all of those stiff clothes." As usual, Anneka chose one of her "literacy club buddies," Sammy, who said, "I thought it was neat that the baby walked to Sarah. Like when I went to camp for a few weeks I came home and my little brother learned how to walk while I was away. So he walked to me when I came home, just like Sarah." Sammy always enjoyed adding a personal story or comment to the discussion—an example of an intertextual link that often helped other children make connections and associations to the story. Rodney then shared his ideas, saying, "I thought it was kind of interesting when she came home or when her family arrived. Like when I was in camp, too, I was happy to see my family after that." Tommy agreed, "Yeah, I thought it was hard for Sarah to have her father go fetch her family." Finally, Claudia made another intertextual link to a different story, saying, "In *Island of the Blue Dolphins*, Karana was scared sometimes, just like Sarah. I think Karana was little older but she also met some people that did not speak her language. That's a really good book, too."

In this group discussion, Lynn assumed the initiator role and started the conversation by asking students to share personal reactions. The discussion took shape as students recalled events from the story. Some participants like Sammy, Rodney, and Claudia connected personal experiences and other texts. Lynn's purpose for the discussion enabled students to assume mostly acceptor, catalyst, and informer roles. The nature of the discussion, however, did not support students assuming more evaluative or critical roles. Sharing their favorite events or aspects left the students with little room for disagreement.

Interpretive authority, as reflected in how students and teachers respond to each other's comments and interpretations, plays an important role in the meaning-construction process. Often overlooked, this hidden influence has the potential to substantiate or detract from what a participant in the literacy event knows and is able to share with others in the group. The structure of the discussion, the place where meaning is thought to reside, and the discourse roles assumed determine whether students and teachers have the authority to state if their interpretations are valid, questionable, or irrelevant. Those perceived to have interpretive authority are often able to suggest a particular topic of discussion, as well as evaluate and judge others' responses. For more information and resources about interpretive and shared authority, see Box 5.2.

Strategies to Encourage Interpretive and Shared Authority

Teachers cognizant of the multiple sources of meaning and the ways in which students interpret texts, tasks, and each other invite alternative structures for meaning making. These alternative structures are somewhat buried from view, but when put in place and acted on, students and teachers can use them to broaden their own understandings of texts and literacy events.

Questions to Encourage Shared Authority

Questions are a natural part of literature discussions and other events. Interpretive and critical questions encourage students to adopt discourse roles beyond that of the responder. A common strategy focused on generating a range of questions is the Question-Answer Relationship (QAR) strategy (Raphael, 1982, 1986). To implement QAR, the teacher first constructs questions that fit into the four categories:

- Right There: The question asks for information that is explicitly found in the text;

Box 5.2
Resources Related to Interpretive and Shared Authority

Flint, A.S. (2000). Know-It-Alls, Identifiers, Defenders, and Solidifiers (KIDS): Examining interpretive authority in literacy events. *Reading Research and Instruction, 39,* 119–134.

Hartman, D. (1994). The intertextual links of readers using multiple passages: A postmodern/semiotic/cognitive view of meaning making. In R.B. Ruddell, M.R. Ruddell, & H. Singer (Eds.), *Theoretical models and processes of reading* (4th ed.; pp. 616–636). Newark, DE: International Reading Association.

Rosenblatt, L.M. (1978). *The reader, the text, the poem: The transactional theory of the literary work.* Carbondale, IL: Southern Illinois University Press.

Rosenblatt, L.M. (1994). The transactional theory of reading and writing. In R.B. Ruddell, M.R. Ruddell, & H. Singer (Eds.), *Theoretical models and processes of reading* (4th ed.; pp. 1057–1092). Newark, DE: International Reading Association.

Ruddell, R.B., & Unrau, N. (1997). The role of responsive teaching in focusing reader intention and developing reader motivation. In J.T. Guthrie and A. Wigfield (Eds.), *Reading engagement: Motivating readers through integrated instruction* (pp. 102–127). Newark, DE: International Reading Association.

Wooten, D. (2000). *Valued voices: An interdisciplinary approach to teaching and learning.* Newark, DE: International Reading Association

- Think and Search: The question is text-based, but the response is inferred from a variety of sources in the text;

- Author and You: The question asks for information that is a combination of the text and students' personal experiences and knowledge; and

- On My Own: The question asks for information that is primarily from the students' background and experiences.

The range of questions enables students to access a variety of meaning sources, thereby influencing and increasing the types of discourse roles assumed during the discussion. Figure 13 on page 108 exemplifies how Lynn used the QAR strategy for the literature selection *The Great Kapok Tree: A Tale of the Amazon Rain Forest* (Cherry, 1990).

When students have the opportunity to respond to questions that encourage them to speculate, challenge, defend, and inquire, the discussion moves to a higher level of critical thinking and reflecting. These types of questions provide students with the necessary space to venture

Figure 13
QAR Strategy

Right There
Identify the four layers of the rain forest.

Author and You
If you were an ocelot, in which layer of the rain forest would you live?

Think and Search
What purpose does the canopy serve in the rain forest?

On My Own
Compare the layers of the rain forest with the layers of another habitat.

a response or interpretation. Interpretive questions encourage students to connect background experiences, world knowledge, and imagination with the story. As students read and discuss important issues in the story, they begin to consider the delicate relationships between texts, tasks, and each other in their community of learners.

Scaffolding Discourse Roles Through the "Fishbowl" Strategy

The fishbowl strategy (Scherer, 1997) is one that enables teachers and students to reflect on the types of discourse roles that are present in a discussion. To initiate the strategy, the teacher asks a group of four or five students to sit in a close circle, while the remaining students sit around the group—students in the center are, in essence, in the fishbowl. Students observing the conversation enter into the discussion when appropriate. The larger audience group listens carefully and evaluates the small group discussion on content and interaction patterns. Through extended conversation, the observers share their impressions and comments. This particular strategy is designed to make more explicit some of the implicit patterns and influences in the classroom.

The following conversation about *The Mouse and the Motorcycle* by the fourth graders illustrated the fishbowl strategy. At this point in the discussion, students were wondering about the relationship between Ralph and Keith, and why they are friends:

Marcy: Why does Keith let Ralph ride the motorcycle?

Clark: Because he is responsible.

[Students all talk at once.]

Elaine: Because he is probably afraid.

Clark: He's probably afraid that if the mouse can talk, what else can he do. Or he's just a really nice kid.

Elaine: Yeah.

Marcy: I think that Ralph, um, rides the motorcycle, that Keith lets Ralph ride the motorcycle because he trusted him.

Clark: No, Keith didn't trust Ralph.

Marcy: Because he trusted Ralph.

Amy: What evidence? What makes you think he trusted Ralph?

Marcy: Ralph said he wouldn't let anything happen to the motorcycle.

Amy: Okay, so he is taking him on his word.

Elizabeth: He wants Keith to think he is really responsible.

A number of students were engaged in this discussion. Marcy initiated a question that encouraged others to consider responses that brought in both textual and personal understandings. The observers of the activity (those in the larger audience group) discussed the types of roles that the students in the fishbowl assumed, as well as where the meanings were based. A follow-up discussion about what the students observed occurred when their observations become public and explicit. The fishbowl strategy is designed to help students consider other discourse roles they might assume in literacy events.

Talking About Interpretive and Shared Authority

Conversations with students about interpretive and shared authority play an important role in the meaning-construction process. When is text an authority? When are peers' experiences and world knowledge

---

Box 5.3
Questions to Ask About Interpretive and Shared Authority

- Why do readers sometimes go back to the story to find information? Why is it important to think about what the author has told us?

- When do you, as a reader, find it helpful to make connections to other sources, such as other stories, experiences, and movies?

- When do you, as a group member, find the connections others make helpful to meaning making?

- What types of links do you like to use most often?

---

valued as contributions to the group's understanding of text? As teachers and students work together to construct shared interpretations, there should be opportunities to explicitly acknowledge when intertextual links foster meaning making, and how these links support new directions for the conversation. Facilitating this type of conversation not only expands what is perceived as appropriate in the discussion, but also encourages students to consider times when a peer's response has not been accepted as valid and viable to meaning making. Articulating understandings related to interpretive and shared authority provides students with insights into how to construct negotiated interpretations of texts with others. We have provided some guiding questions to ask about interpretive and shared authority in Box 5.3.

Reflection Point 5.3

As you consider your students and curriculum, select one of the instructional strategies outlined in this chapter to implement into your literacy program. Observe how various children negotiate and construct meaning when the answer is not in the text.

Interpretive and shared authority shift among participants depending on how literacy events are structured in classroom settings. At various times in various discussions, Lynn, Jane, and Kathy made it possible for students to assume alternative discourse roles and share connections to other experiences and texts. In doing so, they expanded the discussion to recognize and honor the multiple sources of meaning that are available in any given discussion. As teachers and students initiate and participate in meaningful discussion of texts, it is important to be aware of how the implicit and hidden nature of interpretive authority contributes to the meaning-making process. It is also important to recognize that each student brings to the discussion valuable comments that further support understandings of the text.

The next chapter brings together the three hidden influences and explores the idea of flexibility within stance, social positioning, and interpretive authority. We will pursue what happens when literacy events are narrowly conceived or broadly defined by the teachers and students. How different might the events look if flexibility is in place and multiple responses are appreciated?

Reflection Point 5.4

1. In what ways have the ideas presented in this chapter expanded your understanding of how children negotiate and construct text?

2. What insights have you gained by observing your learners seek answers in multiple sources of meaning?

3. How will you encourage your students to value peers' experiences and knowledge?

Chapter 6

Broadening Our Understandings: Flexibility Within the Hidden Influences

Brandi and Claudia are sitting next to each other in the computer lab publishing their Halloween stories. Claudia asks Brandi how she decides on chapters in her stories, because for the students, determining chapters in their stories is an important step in the writing process.

Brandi: *I like to write chapter stories.*

Claudia: *Yeah, me too, but I am not sure how to divide my story up into chapters.*

Brandi: *Oh, I decide to make my chapters when I get to the end of the page.*

Claudia: *But what if you are not finished saying what you want to say? Do you go on to the next page or make a new chapter?*

Brandi: *Well, it depends. If I get to the end of the page and I am at the end of the sentence, then that's it. That is the end of my chapter, so I start a new chapter on the top of the next page.*

Claudia: *So do you make the chapters as you write your story or as you type it?*

Brandi: *As I type it, usually.*

Claudia: *Oh, okay, thanks. I like to make the chapters as I write. If the characters in my story go on another adventure or*

112

meet someone new then I make a new chapter. But then
sometimes when I publish my story the chapters end in
the middle of the page.

Brandi: *Well, I guess that's okay.*

Claudia: *Yeah, I think so. Ms. Fike said it was okay and it was up*
to me to decide where the chapter ends.

Brandi: *Do you give new titles to your chapters or just number*
them?

Claudia: *Usually I try to think of a new title. If the girls are going*
to the store, I'll title the chapter "A Trip to the Store" or
something like that. How 'bout you?

Brandi: *Well, sometimes if I can think of a title, I will write it,*
but otherwise, I just put "Chapter 1, 2" and you know…

Claudia: *But I like to give a hint of what is going to happen in the*
chapter.

Brandi: *I know, but sometimes I like to figure it out myself.*

This discussion invited the girls to access background knowledge and
share personal understandings of the concept of "chapters" in the writing
process. Both girls enjoyed reading chapter books, and they understood
the significance of chapters in these books. While they talked through the
writing process, the girls negotiated and co-constructed their ideas and
understandings about writing chapters. Implicitly, Lynn encouraged the
girls to make decisions on their own. With ease, the girls relied on their
own source of authority to make the final decision in determining where
chapters begin and how to title them. How these two students came to
work together and value the ways in which each decided on chapters re-
lates to both social positioning and interpretive authority.

One morning Michelle and Elaine have the opportunity to work to-
gether on a skill activity sheet for Chapter Three of Island of the Blue
Dolphins. *As the two girls answer a series of questions, they summa-*
rize, construct, and negotiate various responses:

Elaine: *So how did the sea otter look? [referring to the first ques-*
tion on the worksheet]

Michelle: *Now Ramo says that Captain Orlov is trimming his beard so it looked the way it did when he first came. And the Aleuts, they all, they all sharpened the long spears and when they were sharpening them [interrupted by the classroom phone ringing].... So now we are going to write.*

Elaine: *Okay, so describe the sea otter... The sea otter was brown or gray?*

The girls refer to the book to locate the answer.

Michelle: *Here it is. It's on the first page of Chapter Three.*

Elaine: *So it says…*

Michelle: *When it's swimming it looks like a seal, but it is really very different.*

Elaine: *What? When it's swimming it looks like a…*

Michelle: *...seal, but it's really very different.*

At this point, the girls stop talking and move to writing their answers on the activity sheet. They are both quiet. About a minute later, Michelle turns to talk to Amy.

Michelle: *Elaine is looking at my paper and copying me and she will get into trouble.*

Elaine: *Nuh-uh, I'm copying the book. Let me see what you put. I'm not going to copy.*

Michelle: *What did you put?*

Elaine: *I put when it is swimming it looks like a seal but it is really very different. It has a shorter nose than a seal. It has little webbed feet instead of what?*

Michelle: *Flippers.*

Both girls immediately referred to the chapter to answer the first question about the description of the sea otter. When Michelle located the answer, she commented that it was on the first page of Chapter Three and began to write her answer. Elaine, not as quick to get started as

Michelle, glanced over at Michelle's paper, which at this point had an almost complete answer for question number one. Michelle interpreted the glance as a copying glance and reacted. It seemed that for Michelle it was appropriate to construct and share a negotiated oral response, but not a written one. It was also acceptable to copy information from the text as revealed by Michelle's written response and Elaine's defense of her actions.

This brief interchange and the respective written responses to the questions show how two readers may make public and visible different literary stances, and how sources of meaning may also be flexible and varied. Both girls referred to the text before answering the first three questions. The source of meaning resided mostly in the text, particularly for Michelle. Her oral and written responses demonstrated that she was able to accurately locate information in the text, and could share what the characters had said in the text. Elaine had infused a more aesthetic response to the questions, and she showed this in her discussion of the questions. She did not directly transfer the language of the text to her paper; rather she used her own words, reflective of her personality. In response to question number two—"Why didn't Karana like the Aleuts hunting the sea otters? What did she think would happen to them?"— Elaine wrote, "She didn't like the Aleuts because the sea otters would be gone by the time the Aleuts go back to their village. She always plays with them. The sea otters are her best friends." This response demonstrated that Elaine was able to construct an interpretation that reflected a negotiation between text and reader.

In this chapter we explore the interrelated nature of stance, social positioning, and interpretive authority, and what the collective impact of these influences may be for meaning making. We wonder how teachers and students successfully negotiate among the three, and if there is some flexibility in doing so. What does it mean to be flexible in assuming various stances toward literature? How does flexibility in recognizing sources of meaning contribute to one's understanding of the text, task, context, and each other?

Reflection Point 6.1 _____

Reflect on a recent literature response activity in your classroom.

1. Describe the event itself and how flexible you were in your planning and implementation of the event.

2. What impact does flexibility have in creating meaningful literacy experiences for your students?

Embracing Flexibility Within the Hidden Influences

The teachers and students in these two classrooms participated in a wide range of literacy events. Transacting with text and making sense of text resulted in the co-mingling of ideas between readers, texts, and contexts. As teachers and students came together during literacy events, they shared their own constructions of meaning and negotiated new insights not yet presented. Throughout the events, we noticed how the hidden influences varied in levels of significance as participants engaged in reading and writing. In some events, the literary stance appeared to make a difference, while in other events social positioning contributed to or detracted from constructing meaning. However, no matter what the event, it was the teachers' or students' abilities to flexibly navigate among the influences that seemed to have the greatest impact on meaning making.

Flexibility, much like Rosenblatt's efferent/aesthetic literary stance (see Chapter 3), may be positioned on a continuum. Figure 14 extends the work of Flint, Lysaker, Riordan-Karlsson, and Molinelli (1999) to illustrate flexibility as related to the hidden influences. At one end of the continuum, teachers and students embody a flexible perspective toward texts, tasks, and each other when they consider multiple sources of meaning amidst a variety of tasks and among various event participants. In these instances, we may see teachers and students involved in research projects using the Internet.

Figure 14
Continuum of Flexibility Within the Hidden Influences

Stance, social positioning, and interpretive authority are perceived as flexible, dynamic, and open to alternative interpretations	Stance, social positioning, and interpretive authority are perceived as rigid, static, and closed to alternative interpretations
More Flexible	Less Flexible

⟵ ———————————————————————————————— ⟶

STANCE What are my purposes for the event? How might these purposes change as the event is enacted?

SOCIAL POSITIONING How do students enter into events? How might the evaluative criteria reflect other aspects?

INTERPRETIVE AUTHORITY Who is determining the validity and viability of a response? How might alternative sources of meaning be explored?

Technology enhances flexibility in how students respond and interact with information because of the nonlinear nature of Web sites. In Lynn's class, for example, students participated in the Cyber-Travels of Flat Stanley Project. When Lynn first read *Flat Stanley* (Brown, 1996), she and the students adopted a predominantly aesthetic stance. This entertaining story is about a young boy, Stanley Lambchop, who wakes up to discover that he has been flattened to the width of one-half inch when his bulletin board falls on him. He wanted to visit a friend in California, so he made the best of a bad situation, folded himself, and mailed himself there. Although this story has been around for years, many teachers and students are using technology to document his travels. Students send Flat Stanley through their electronic mail to friends in different places and then students and teachers from across the United States respond by contributing information and photographs from their town and state to Web

sites such as The Cyber-Travels of Flat Stanley (http://seamonkey.ed.
asu.edu/~hixson/stanley/index.html) or Flat Stanley Project (http://flat-
stanley.enoreo.on.ca).

The children enjoyed hearing of Stanley's travels, and they shared
their own personal stories of traveling. The project, however, took on a
more efferent stance when students began researching information about
their town and state. Social positioning and interpretive authority also
shifted among the students as new information was shared and posted on
the Web site. Students used their evaluative criteria to form collaborative
working groups, and various participants revealed how they navigated the
Internet in alternative ways. Inviting students to explore and examine information through different routes on the Internet exemplifies a position
on the more flexible end of the continuum of flexibility.

Conversely, teachers and students may assume a more inflexible perspective toward texts, tasks, and each other, and they may not be able to
entertain the possibility of alternatives in the meaning-construction
process. This lack of flexibility may lead to narrowly defined ways of engaging within literacy events. When this occurs, there is little room to accept a divergent interpretation or way of engaging with a text. Often
teachers and students tend to be less flexible when there are pressures or
outside constraints, such as standardized tests or district expectations to
demonstrate understanding and knowledge in particular categories. Although standards play an important role in our educational system, it is
also important to establish a curriculum that is not solely driven by them.

Literacy Moments on the Flexible End of the Continuum

Opportunities for the students and teachers in the two classroom communities to position themselves toward the more flexible end of the hidden influence continuum appeared in a variety of experiences and events.
The teachers assumed a range of instructional stances throughout the literacy events, and they encouraged students to consider how different
interpretations might be possible depending on background knowledge
and experience. Moreover, the teachers and students opened the discussions and conversations to include the voices and experiences of many.

Flexibility in how the meaning-construction process was conceptualized and orchestrated was closely aligned with the teachers' beliefs

about literacy and learning. Recall that Jane and Kathy wanted students to focus on personal connections with the characters in the books they read. This aspect of their belief system established an important connection among personal experiences, engagement, and comprehension of text. Amy also believed that the personal connections could facilitate meaning making. As the fourth-grade book club group came together to read and discuss their literature selections, the students shaped the discussion to reflect a loosely constituted conversation, with multiple points of view and experiences, rather than a narrowly defined pathway of single answers. The following dialogue illustrates how the book club students offered multiple interpretations and negotiated new understandings of events in *Hundred Penny Box*. At this point in the book and conversation, the students are questioning the decision made by Michael's mom when she insisted on Aunt Dew taking a nap. They also offer brief comments on their beliefs about dying:

Marcy:	I think that Michael's mom should make Aunt Dew [take a nap] because she might not fall asleep at the dinner table.
Robert:	She might die in her sleep.
Amy:	I think that would be a big fear of Michael, especially if that hundred penny box is taken away.
Marcy:	I think…
Kelly:	Probably she won't go. The hundred penny box is so special to her.
Robert:	How would she know if it is missing, unless she goes looking for it?
Elaine:	Can't she, can't she say her prayers, "Now I lay me down to sleep"? That one. "And if I should die before I wake, I pray the Lord my soul to take."
Robert:	Yeah, but…[Students begin to interrupt each other, and it is difficult to hear anyone.]
Amy:	You think she should say that prayer?
Robert:	Michael will come into the room…
Elaine:	I don't know the long one.
Kelly:	I don't know the ones in English, 'cause I say them in Spanish. I went to CCD in Spanish.

The students' beliefs about dying and elderly relatives were revealed in the ways in which they talked about Aunt Dew saying prayers and how she might die if the hundred penny box is taken away from her. Their aesthetic stance toward the story indicated that they were interested in better understanding the emotions and motivations of the characters.

Notice, too, how the students adopted various discourse roles—roles or positions within the conversation that are determined by its content and structure. Marcy made a statement that suggested she was assuming a catalyst role, while others were informers and inquisitors (review Chapter 5 for an explanation of these roles and others). Broadening the discourse roles enabled students to construct discussions reflective of loosely managed conversations in which no one person was in charge. In this example, students shared their personal connections and the interpretive authority to validate and honor these connections.

Moreover, consider how students were positioned within their group— the students worked together, bringing in ideas and understandings from their own lives. Absent on this particular day, however, was Elizabeth, with whom many of the students struggled in terms of social interaction. Had she been present in the discussion, it is difficult to know if Robert or Clark would have made any comments that would have reflected their authority to discount her interpretations and ideas. It is highly possible that these two would have assumed evaluator roles, and would have negatively evaluated Elizabeth when she attempted to share an idea or comment.

On a different day, with a different story and a different task, we observed the same students again constructing responses appropriated from personal experiences. Jane and Kathy assigned the students a book report for *Otherwise Known as Sheila, the Great*. The book report, first mentioned in Chapter 2 (see page 35) was formatted to include characters, setting, three events, climax, and conclusion. Students wrote responses for each category, and they drew pictures. The teachers indicated that it was important to record information from the text, and it was important to include personal impressions and knowledge into the report. This flexibility between factual information and personal interpretations provided the students with opportunities for creative and interesting responses.

Marcy's book report relied heavily on textual information. Her responses were detailed accounts of the story, and she took this opportunity to demonstrate her ability to recall specific facts. Marcy even included quotes directly transcribed from the text. What follows is Marcy's book report for *Otherwise Known as Sheila, the Great*:

Characters:
Sheila and her sister Libby lived in an apartment in New York City. Sheila is very snotty and she says that she's not afraid of anything but she is. Libby is boy crazy. All she talks about is boys. She also shows off. Libby's favorite thing to do is dance.

Setting:
When Sheila and Libby went to Tarry Town they stayed at the Egrans' house. Sheila expected a room prettier than the room she had. Sheila wasn't happy with the room that she was staying in because there were models, equipment, and trophies. There was a blanket on top of the bed that said, "Camp Kenabee." Sheila expected a room with a yellow rug with a red rose on it and the bed would be a canopy bed and the curtains would have lots of lace.

Event I:
When Sheila was in the driveway she met a girl named Mouse. She said, "hi" to Sheila. They both started to talk to each other. Mouse had a yo-yo in her hand and did some tricks. Sheila said that where she lives, yo-yos are for babies. Mouse said that the yo-yo she has is called the Duncan Imperial.

Event II:
Sheila took swimming lessons at the pool. At the pool Sheila met her swimming teacher, Marty. Sheila told Marty that she didn't want to put her face in the water.

Event III:
Sheila and Mouse went on a hayride. It was very dark outside and Sheila thought that a storm was coming so she hid in the hay. Mouse told Sheila that there was no storm. Sheila started to hear some noises. She thought it might be the headless horseman. Sheila was worrying about going into the woods and that the wolves might try to attack.

Climax:
At the end of the summer Marty gave Sheila a swimming test. She had to jump in the deep end of the pool and swim across. She jumped in and started to swim across. Marty told Sheila that if she wanted to get out he would pull her out. He didn't pull her out. She swam across the pool.

Conclusion:
Sheila had a going away barbeque because it was time to go home to New York City. Sheila invited Marty and Mouse. Sheila's sister Libby invited her friend. At the barbeque Mouse asked Sheila, "if she was going to come back to Tarry Town." Mouse told Sheila that she will tell of [sic] the

Egrans that you got the letter. Jennifer's friend, Mumford [a dog], comes back. Sheila is not that afraid of Jennifer's friend, so when Jennifer's friend comes by she just stands still.

In contrast, Clark's responses to the book report demonstrated that the sources of meaning for him were both in the text and within a negotiation among peers. He used the text to identify three characters in the story: Mouse, Sheila, and Libby. His descriptions, however, were generated from discussions held prior to writing the responses. He wrote about Sheila being snotty, a common sentiment among those in the literature discussion group. He also suggested that Libby was boy crazy. This comment stems from the brainstorming activity, where in response to Jane's request to describe Libby, Marcy said, "she likes boys." When Clark wrote about Tarry Town being a little town on the Hudson River, he referred to outside and world knowledge. What follows is Clark's book report for *Otherwise Known as Sheila, the Great*.

Characters:
Three characters of the book are Mouse, Sheila, and Libby. Mouse is smart, and she likes to play. Sheila is snotty and tries to show off too much. Libby thinks she is the best person in the world and is boy crazy.

Setting:
One of the setting [sic] for the story was Tarry Town. It is a little town on the Hudson River. The kids talk about the Headless Horseman. And they have a swimming pool.

Event I:
Sheila is learning to swim. She is very afraid that she'll sink and drown.

Event II:
Sheila and her friends are fixing the models that they broke so they don't get into trouble.

Event III:
Sheila is on a hayride. She is up in the front of the wagon. She won't get out of the hay because there is a storm.

Climax:
Sheila has conquered her fear. She has taken the swimming test. She now knows how to swim.

Conclusion:
Sheila is leaving town. Her family is having a barbeque. Sheila found that Jennifer's friend's name was Mumford.

The book reports by Marcy and Clark provide glimpses as to how the teachers initially established some flexibility in their purposes and intentions. Because of this, the students were able to construct different yet appropriate responses. Marcy relied on the text to construct her responses, while Clark was willing to use the text and negotiate responses heard in discussions. Both students received high marks for their book reports because the teachers recognized that it was possible to approach the task from differing vantage points.

Less Flexible Moments in Literacy Events

There were times, however, when the teachers and students were positioned on the more inflexible side of the continuum, partly due to the teachers' concerns about comprehending text in a particular way. A significant number of literature discussions facilitated by Jane and Kathy were focused on particular aspects of the story and seemed to be aligned along the less flexible end of the continuum. This may be attributed to their apprehension about expectations in the fourth-grade curriculum. *Island of the Blue Dolphins* was chosen specifically because it introduced students to California history. Jane commented to Amy that it was important for the students to focus on comprehension because she felt they would not get anything out of the story or understand what was going on otherwise. With this in mind, these two teachers were quite deliberate in attending to information located in the text. The following excerpt demonstrates a more limited perspective on what an appropriate response might be. Specifically, Kathy asked students to think about what the island looks like because they were to draw a picture of the island on the front cover of their literature study folders.

Kathy:	What do you think the island looks like? The description is in the book. It is very detailed.
Elaine:	It looks like a dolphin on its side.
Kathy:	On the cover of my book it shows dolphins jumping in the water. What else might be jumping or swimming around in the water by the edge of the island?
Brady:	Fish.
Kathy:	Fish, what else?
Jackson:	Otter.

Kathy:	Otter, what else? Another animal. There's a lot of them around. What else? Seals. They also mention seals. Any one of those things can be around the island. It needs to be a picture of the island. It needs to have water around it and things in the water. It needs to be neat and colored in. Your name goes on the bottom. You need to use the entire sheet of paper. I don't want a tiny picture in the middle.
Elaine:	And then the rest is water and mountains.
Kathy:	The island needs to be big. You can put things on the island.
Elaine:	Like coconut trees.
Kathy:	You might have the girl on the island. You might have the twisted trees. What else might you have on the island?
Elaine:	A big rock.
Kathy:	The big rock might be on the island. Clark, what else?
Elaine:	Teepees.
Clark:	The village.
Kathy:	The village might be on the island. The girls, the village. What else?
Kelly:	Can you put a teepee on it?
Kathy:	Did it say teepees?
Kelly:	Tents.
Elizabeth:	Houses.
Kathy:	They don't live in houses. What did it say they lived in?

This dialogue continued with Kathy asking students to recall specific information to use to draw their pictures of the island. In this interaction, there was little flexibility in what constituted an appropriate response. Elaine ventured a response of "teepee" when trying to think about what might be on the island, and Elizabeth tried "houses." Both responses did not match what Kathy had in mind and were therefore not accepted as contributing to the conversation. As students searched for the appropriate responses, their discourse roles were reduced to that of responder. They were unable to consider alternative ways of participating in the discussion or activity. Moreover, by limiting flexibility in what might be a viable response, the students had fewer opportunities to assume authority within the discussion.

More prescribed and rigid engagement with text also occurred in Lynn's classroom when students completed skill sheets after reading particular books. Lynn explained that there were certain skills that needed to be targeted and there were different ways of addressing those skills, including the use of comprehension worksheets to assess literal comprehension. "The *Julian Tales* lends itself really well to comprehension work because it has short little chapters and they can read it and then answer the questions," she said. Lynn explained to the students that it was okay to have the same answer if they discussed it with their partner and came to the same conclusion; however, they each needed to complete a worksheet. In the following exchange, Tommy and Jennifer read the chapter, "I Learn Firefighting," and fill in their comprehension worksheet. Again, there is limited discussion and no space to construct alternative responses.

Tommy: Okay, the first question asks, "Why does Julian want to be like Smokey the Bear?" Well, that's easy. So he doesn't get in trouble so much.

Jennifer: Yeah, it says right here, wait, um…he wants to put out sparks of trouble like a forest fire right at the beginning.

Tommy: Okay, are you finished writing? Um, the next question says, "What was the first 'spark' that started Julian's problem with Huey?"

Jennifer: He called him a scaredy cat.

Tommy: Yeah, that's right. Okay, the number three says, "How did Huey feel about the way Julian was treating him?"

Jennifer: He felt bad. He did not like to be treated like that.

Tommy: I'm just gonna say he felt very sad.

Jennifer: Okay, I wrote a little more.

Tommy: Okay these last few questions are asking us how we feel, so we might have different answers. It says, "How do you feel when you see someone you love does well at something?"

Jennifer: Oh, I would feel really happy for them.

Tommy: Me too, 'cause I love to see my friends do well at something.

In this interchange there was limited flexibility in stance, social positioning, and interpretive authority. The source of meaning mostly resided in the text, except for the last question in which the children were asked how they felt. Throughout the event, the students adopted a predominantly efferent stance with a slight fluctuation to an aesthetic stance at times. The purpose and goal of the activity clearly dictated the adopted stance and how the children positioned themselves within the event.

Reflection Point 6.2

A number of vignettes have been shared throughout various chapters.

1. Return to a favorite excerpt from each of the classrooms, and determine the level of flexibility among the teachers and students.

2. What elements of the event signified a particular level of flexibility?

3. Now think about your own classroom practices. What elements of a particular event exemplify your flexibility or lack thereof?

In the two classrooms we observed, the teachers and students enacted many literacy events that can be positioned at various points along the continuum of flexibility. Some of the events were structured so that multiple interpretations and ways of participating in the event were possible. Other events had the characteristics of a less flexible and limited perspective. Still others indicated that the levels of flexibility among teachers and students were variable. It is important for teachers and students to consider the impact of flexibility on the hidden influences, as well as on the meaning-making process. The interpretations and ideas negotiated as a result of flexibility and openness to alternative stances and sources of meaning lead to richer and more complex insights of teaching, learning, and literacy processes.

Strategies to Enhance Flexibility Within the Hidden Influences

As seen in the vignettes and excerpts in this chapter, teachers' instructional stances and purposes for the events played a significant role in how literacy events were structured within the classroom setting and the types of responses deemed acceptable to meaning construction. Students responded to these stances as they constructed interpretations of texts, tasks, and each other. The interplay among teachers' and students' stances suggests that flexibility of the hidden influences may contribute to a broadening of how literacy events are defined and constituted. In the next section, instructional strategies are provided to facilitate this notion of flexibility.

QuICS

A particularly effective strategy for expanding one's flexibility toward multiple stances and responses is QuICS (Lewison & Heffernan, 2000). Developed by Lee Heffernan, a third-grade teacher, QuICS encourages children to respond to text in different ways. Using this strategy, children record their questions (Qu), interesting points (I), connections (C), and surprises (S) as they read a story. Their responses can be recorded on colored notecards—such as yellow for questions, green for interests, blue for connections, and pink for surprises—and the notecards can be placed in the book at the various discussion points. Encourage students to ask questions that are authentic and meaningful. Interesting points are those places in the text that a student finds intriguing and worthy of discussion. Connections include personal experiences, other texts and media, world knowledge, and any other source of information. (See Chapter 5 for discussion of these intertextual links.) The surprises are composed of those character actions, events, or outcomes that the reader does not expect.

After students record their thoughts, they should share these notes with others in the discussion group. Because each reader will transact with the text in different ways, the QuICS will reflect a broad range of interests and background experiences. QuICS can be used to facilitate the adoption of various stances toward the texts, as well as to validate multi-

Figure 15
Example of QuICS Notes

QUESTION
Why did Karana choose to stay on the island when she could have been rescued?

INTERESTING POINT
I would have been so lonely if I had to be there by myself and did not know for how long.

CONNECTIONS
Reminds me of seeing the sea otters; Courage of Sarah Noble; and not knowing other people's language

SURPRISES
I was surprised that Karana was eventually rescued and lived in Santa Barbara.

ple sources of meaning and discourse roles. An example for *Island of the Blue Dolphins* is provided in Figure 15.

The QuICS activity may be extended by asking students to select one of the ideas on a notecard to follow up with further discussion, writing, and/or research. In some cases, the research and discussion become the beginnings of inquiry projects.

Broadening the Selection of Books to Read

In recent years, there has been a growing interest in students reading books that address significant social issues. Harste et al. (2000) describe these as "social issues books." These literature selections encourage children to view issues from multiple perspectives and to ask why some groups of people have been marginalized. Social issues books also do not have the common "they lived happily ever after" ending of children's books, but rather support readers in constructing their own endings to the complex story lines. When students read these stories, they have ample opportunity to address divergent and alternative points of view. The realistic nature of these literature selections encourages students to bring their own experiences and interpretations to the conversation. In doing so, they may interpret and position their responses and those of others in multiple ways. Box 6.1 contains sample titles of books in this social issues genre.

Social issues books encourage students to move beyond traditional literature discussion and take steps toward social action and critical literacy. It is important that students know not only how to decode and make meaning, but also to understand how language positions who we are and who we may become (Harste et al., 2000).

Box 6.1
Social Issues Books for Discussions

Picture Books:

Browne, A. (1998). *Voices in the park*. New York: DK Publishing.

Bunting, E. (1998). *So far from the sea*. New York: Clarion.

Bunting, E. (1998). *Your move*. New York: Harcourt Brace.

Lorbiecki, M. (1996). *Just one flick of the finger*. New York: Dial Books.

Lorbiecki, M. (1998). *Sister Anne's hands*. New York: Dial Books.

McGuffee, M. (1996). *The day the earth was silent*. Bloomington, IN: Inquiring Voices Press.

Miller, W. (1998). *The bus ride*. New York: Lee & Low.

Mora, P. (1997). *Tomas and the library lady*. New York: Knopf.

Shange, N. (1997). *White wash*. New York: Walker & Company.

Chapter Books:

Fleishman, P. (1997). *Seedfolks*. New York: HarperCollins.

Fleishman, P. (1998). *Whirligig*. New York: Henry Holt.

Fletcher, R. (1998). *Flying solo*. New York: Clarion.

Hesse, K. (1998). *just [sic] Juice*. New York: Scholastic.

Spinelli, J. (1997). *Wringer*. New York: HarperCollins.

Walter, V. (1998). *Making up megaboy*. New York: DK Publishing.

Wolff, V.E. (1998). *Bat 6*. New York: Scholastic.

Save the Last Word for Me

All readers construct interpretations based on their own experiences, other texts, and conversations. A strategy developed by Carolyn Burke titled "Save the Last Word for Me" (see Short & Harste, 1996) encourages multiple perspectives and divergent thinking. This activity demystifies the notion that there is one "right" interpretation.

To engage in "Save the Last Word for Me," students read a story and write the words, phrases, or sentences that captured their attention on slips of paper or index cards, along with the page numbers for easy reference. On the other side of the card, students write what the words, phrases, or sentences mean to them personally. After reading and writing, students arrange their cards in order of importance, and then come together to share their cards. One student begins by reading the quote on his or her card, and the others respond to the quote. The student who read the quote "has the last word" about why that particular phrase or sentence was important based on what he or she wrote on the card and the discussion that just occurred.

Internet Projects

Technology and the Internet increase flexibility in how students respond and interact with information in the classroom. Internet projects can be designed with flexibility of stance and social positioning in mind, either as individual projects, in-class collaborative projects, or class-to-class projects. To complete individual projects, students work alone, which strengthens their research and organization skills. Working individually also enforces responsibility and self-motivation, as well as skills needed in the Information Age.

An in-class collaborative project encourages children to work effectively with others using technology. If you can integrate projects with collaborative groups or cooperative learning groups, make sure each team member has a specific role and responsibility related to the Internet research project. (Boxes 6.3 and 6.4 offer additional resources on technology integration and project sites.)

There are different types and formats of Internet projects. Following are sample descriptions of various ways in which technology may be used in classroom settings.

Information literacy projects. Students choose a subject they would like to research, and they progress through information literacy skills such as locating, analyzing, and organizing the information to effectively communicate new knowledge and understandings. Students can also evaluate their learning and progress in the Internet search.

Curriculum-focused projects. These projects are based on curriculum content areas (such as math, social studies, science) and are designed to enrich a student's knowledge base on a specific subject. Teachers should provide students with a list of Web sites to help them complete

---

Box 6.2
Resources for Integrating Technology

Garfield, G.M., & McDonough, S. (1996). *Creating a technologically literate classroom.* Westminster, CA: Teacher Created Materials.

Haag, T. (1996). *Internet for kids.* Westminster, CA: Teacher Created Materials.

Hayes, D.S. (1995). *Managing technology into the classroom.* Westminster, CA: Teacher Created Materials.

Leu, D.J., & Leu, D.D. (1997). *Teaching with the Internet: Lessons from the classroom.* Norwood, MA: Christopher-Gordon.

Lifter, M.A., & Adams, M.E. (1997). *Integrating technology into the curriculum—primary.* Westminster, CA: Teacher Created Materials.

Sandholtz, J.H. (1997). *Teaching with technology: Creating student-centered classrooms.* New York: Teachers College Press.

Box 6.3
Internet Sites for Project Ideas

Ask Dr. Science: www.ducksbreath.com

Pitsco's Ask an Expert: www.askanexpert.com

The Keypals Project: seamonkey.ed.asu.edu/~hixson/comz/keypalsproject.html

The Center for Improved Engineering and Science Education: k12science.ati.stevens-tech.edu/renie/ciese.html

Classroom Connect: www.classroomconnect.com

CRAYON: www.crayon.net

Cyber-Seuss: www.afn.org/~afn15301/drseuss.html

Cyber-Travels of Flat Stanley: seamonkey.ed.asu.edu/~hixson/stanley/index.html

World Walk Travel Adventure: home.earthlink.net/~earthwalker1

The Global Schoolhouse at Lightspan.Com: www.gsn.org

The Museum of Science, Boston: www.mos.org

their projects. Remind students to keep track of the Web sites they use to complete their projects, similar to a bibliography.

Theme-focused projects. These projects are based on a specific theme to be studied, such as environmental issues, homelessness, or racial inequalities. Projects are supplemented with visits to specific Web sites related to the theme. For example, you may have a social issue theme such as environmental awareness, and students can choose topics to research and extend into class presentations.

Reflection Point 6.3

1. Have you already engaged in an Internet project with your students? If so, please describe the project and its results.

2. If you have not engaged in an Internet project with your students, describe a project you think might be exciting to implement in your classroom to support your curriculum.

Literacy events and practices are multidimensional, nonlinear, and full of complexities. As the possibilities in our world continue to expand, it is crucial that we expand our understandings of what literacy entails and how it may be constructed. Broadening our conceptions of what a particular stance or purpose may be, the ways in which children enter into and participate in such events, and the types of responses and interpretations they construct enables the learning community to enact a literacy curriculum that honors the voices and interests of all. Flexibility in the literacy curriculum encourages teachers and students to bring themselves and their diverse and evolving perspectives into discussions and written examples. Moreover, flexibility allows students to consider the varied positions they can take to better understand their world.

In the final chapter, we continue the discussion of creating technologically rich, socially active curricula that support teachers and students as they make explicit the hidden influences.

Chapter 7

New Directions and Treasures to Consider

On a bright, crisp, November morning in the San Francisco Bay Area, the fourth-grade book club group from Jane and Kathy's classroom heads to the library. There they talk about concerns related to an event in the story: Ralph the mouse contemplates how he will properly pay for the room service he received in the hotel. Amy initiates conversation with a question designed to encourage the children to predict future events.

Amy: *At the end of the chapter it says, "'Don't worry, I'll think of something,' promised Ralph in the grand way he had acquired since he had order up food to the mouse nest." Any predictions of what Ralph is thinking of doing?*

Elaine: *[quick to respond] He's thinking he won't have room service anymore.*

Clark: *Yeah.*

Elaine: *He [Keith] isn't mad anymore.*

Sensing the conversation not taking hold, Amy again asks, "What do you think Ralph is thinking in terms of what he plans to do to tip Keith, because his mom [Ralph's mom] is so worried they're not able to tip him [Keith] properly or pay for the room service?"

Marcy: *Try to get the motorcycle back.*

Clark: *[more aggressively] If I was Keith and Ralph lost my motorcycle, I'd step on him.*

> Elizabeth: *I was thinking he was going downstairs where people put their money down on the table and steal some. [There is quite a bit of dissention on this idea.]*
>
> Kelly: *I don't think Ralph would steal.*
>
> Amy: *Why don't you think Ralph would steal?*
>
> Kelly: *Well, this is a child's book, um, I don't think there would be robbing in it.*
>
> Elaine: *Yeah, I don't think they'll want children trying to do the same thing.*
>
> Marcy: *What I would do is I'd go to the cashier and take—I would take out 20 dollars and I would bring it to Keith, and say "Keith this is the room service money for all the things you've given me."*

This conversation illustrates many possible directions students can take when sharing their understandings of a story. Kelly's interpretation of what children's books entail provides us with insights into this very complexity. Why wouldn't an author include stealing in a story designed for children? Elaine's response of not wanting children to mimic these actions may in some ways serve as a metaphor for what our hopes and intentions are for planned, responsive pedagogy and what we think it means to be insightful. What is appropriate? What materials work best? How do teachers encourage divergent and alternative responses? How do we plan for a responsive curriculum that meets the needs of all students? These questions are a few of those to consider as we seek to better understand the meaning-construction process.

Reflection Point 7.1 _____

Return to some of your earlier reflections and writings.

1. Have your beliefs and understandings related to literacy development changed as you've read this book?

2. How have your instructional decisions and practices shifted?

3. What new goals do you have for yourself and for your students?

4. What new directions will you pursue?

Throughout this book, we have aimed to address those aspects of the meaning-construction process that are implied, hidden, and in many cases buried and invisible to those in the learning community—teachers and children alike. We began our journey by introducing children in two middle level elementary classrooms who shared with us their stories of what it meant to be meaning makers of texts, tasks, and each other in their respective classrooms. Lynn, Jane, and Kathy—the teachers—offered us different ways of conceptualizing literacy practice, from constructing personal connections to sharing in socially mediated contexts. As the teachers and children participated in a vast array of literacy events, we reflected on and responded to the important call for a more complete understanding of how meanings are shared and negotiated on. In doing so, we learned a tremendous amount about what it means to enact a responsive pedagogy that honors the complexity and multiviewed layers of literacy events.

The hidden influences we articulated in the previous chapters include stance, social positioning, and interpretive authority. We refer to them as hidden not because they are unreachable, but rather because their influences on the meaning-construction process may be buried. We highlighted a number of "treasured moments" in the classrooms that addressed the hidden influences being discussed. We treasure these moments because they provide us with greater insight into teaching and learning processes in our classrooms.

Stance, if you recall, set the stage for the literacy event (see Chapter 3). The overarching question was, What purposes and intentions do you have in mind for the texts and tasks in which your students engage? Are they to read with an efferent, information-finding stance, or does the literature encourage a more aesthetic stance? How does being aware of stance determine the types of questions asked and, subsequently, the types of responses received? We also discussed how a misalignment of stance can lead to frustrations and tensions in the meaning-making process.

Chapter 4 addressed how students positioned themselves in the socially mediated contexts teachers provided for them. The evaluative criteria students use to determine viable partners should be taken into consideration while children work together. What criteria are being used to determine partnerships? What role might you as teacher play in establishing effective and productive partnerships? How do we encourage students to develop many different types of partnerships, depending on their needs and established purposes?

The third hidden influence we discussed (see in Chapter 5) was the nature of interpretive authority and the pursuit of alternative sources of meaning. The discourse roles children and teachers assume and the meanings they locate play a significant role in whether responses are perceived as valid and viable to the meaning-construction process. Whoever determines the viability and validity of the response is said to have interpretive authority. The vignettes and dialogues in Chapter 5 exemplify how students assume various discourse roles and what the implications are when multiple sources of meaning are recognized.

We also wondered about the flexibility of the hidden influences. We highlighted moments in the two classrooms in which the teachers—Jane, Kathy, and Lynn—provided opportunities for students to be more and less flexible in their responses and interpretations of the literacy events. We included strategies that can open this notion of flexibility, including the use of Internet projects and books that address social issues.

By sharing the stories and lives of these children and their teachers, we offer possibilities for more effective and insightful teaching. Elaine's comment about the author not wanting children to steal is a reminder that your own instructional practices should not be based on what others do, but rather on what your students tell you to do through their stances, social positions, and use of authority during literacy events. Kelly and Elaine shared the belief that people will copy what they read. This belief may be true of the students of the many teachers who implement predetermined and preplanned instructional practices without carefully considering the hidden influences and the significant roles they play in literacy learning. This, however, is not reflective of students whose educators are mindful of the directions in which their learners are headed.

Moving Toward a Technology-Rich, Social Action Curriculum

What directions do we, as teachers and researchers, pursue? How do we remain responsive to the hidden influences while recognizing the ever-broadening conception of what it means to be literate in the 21st century? These new beliefs and understandings about literacy require us to constantly refocus and reframe how we participate and engage with literacy. Our boundaries are widening. We will need to create new maps to follow for the 21st-century treasure hunts. Technology, in all of its current and future forms, enables us to establish learning communities near and far, and to imagine others. Jonassen (2000) talks about technology as "mindtools," which are "computer-based tools and learning environments that have been adapted or developed to function as intellectual partners with the learner in order to engage and facilitate critical thinking and higher order learning" (p. 9).

The projects Lynn's students engaged in (such as The Cyber-Travels of Flat Stanley, composing on the computer, and researching the candy factory) illustrate how technology is a mindtool. Internet projects and searches support our belief about how children learn through interactions with others—constructing and negotiating shared understandings. These interactions and collaborations across borders, both political and intellectual, empower students to navigate their own learning—to make relevant and salient their questions, wonderings, and concerns. By using the tools of technology, we not only foster functional literacy—that which is related to reading and writing skills needed to function in an industrial/informational world—but also critical literacy. Critical literacy encourages those in the learning community to address issues of justice and equity, to reflect on the systems of meaning and the groups that people belong to. Access to the Internet and technology enables teachers and students to open new doors, to think critically, analytically, and creatively in new genres and venues. Box 7.1 (see page 138) offers additional resources for connecting technology and literacy.

Box 7.1
Resources for Thinking About Technology in Literacy

Cummins, J., & Sayers, D. (1995). _Brave new schools: Challenging cultural illiteracy through global learning networks._ New York: St. Martin's Press.

Jonassen, D.H. (1999). _Computers as mindtools for schools: Engaging critical thinking_ (2nd ed.). Englewood Cliffs, NJ: Merrill.

Jonassen, D.H., Peck, K.L., & Wilson, B.G., (1999). _Learning with technology: A constructivist approach._ Englewood Cliffs, NJ: Merrill.

Wepner, S.B., Valmont, W.J., & Thurlow, R. (2000). _Linking literacy and technology: A guide for K–8 classrooms._ Newark, DE: International Reading Association.

Reflection Point 7.2

1. What role does technology currently play in your classroom?

2. How might you use technology as a mindtool for your students?

3. How will you transform your students into lifelong learners?

Along with using the tools of technology, ways of teaching literacy are also expanded when we encourage conversations related to social issues and critical literacy. The openness and flexibility with which social issues books are introduced into the curriculum contribute to reframing our views on teaching and learning. These books address such concerns as poverty, violence, environmental issues, homelessness, class, race, and gender. Jane talked about wanting students to personally connect with the characters, and how she might have more success if the issues the characters faced were ones the students could recognize in their own lives. Over a century ago, Dewey (1897) talked about establishing a relevant curriculum when he noted, "I believe that the school [literacy instruction] must represent present life—life as real and vital to the child as that which he carries on in the home, in the neighborhood, or on the playground" (p. 78). If our goals are to implement a relevant and mindful literacy program, it is necessary that teachers and students engage with texts that present multiple perspectives and address real-life issues and dilemmas (Flint, 2000).

Many teachers are working toward this goal. Recently, Amy observed a multiage K–2 classroom in which the teacher read the story *Teammates* (Golenbach, 1990). This story, about Jackie Robinson becoming the first African American player in major league baseball, addresses racial prejudice. In the book, Pee Wee Reese, a white player on the team, supports and accepts Jackie as a player and as a teammate. The children in this classroom responded to the story by sharing their own personal experiences and knowledge of racial prejudice. Issues related to fairness, apartheid, understanding, and discrimination were all raised in the conversation. The teacher's flexibility in hearing the many interpretations and honoring all the voices in the conversation contributed to the success and meaningfulness of the discussion. Many teachers are uncomfortable with and hesitant to read about and discuss these significant social issues, particularly with young children. What is being demonstrated, however, is the power of these books and stories to spark discussions that children and teachers care about.

For this teacher of a multiage classroom, the conversation was compelling. She was surprised by the many issues that children brought up. She now hopes to have students initiate and participate in social action projects that make a difference in their school and local communities. A book by Carol Edelsky (1999) offers readers examples and stories of teachers enacting a critical literacy curriculum. Based on Edelsky's recommendations, which have been adapted from Patterson (1994), characteristics of critical curriculum that teachers may want to consider are outlined in Box 7.2 on page 140.

A socially just, critical literacy curriculum—much like a technology-integrated curriculum—has the potential to demonstrate how the influences of stance, social positioning, and interpretive authority can become visible and explicit in a literacy event. Students engage in conversations that may have a significant impact on the ways in which they participate in society. By addressing tough issues that explore differences in culture, language, history, class, gender, and race, students are able to access experiences and knowledge that, in turn, supports them as they become active and responsible members of the community and the world.

Box 7.2
Characteristics of Critical Curriculum

- Contains no (or few) exercises—curriculum should be authentic and relevant to the lives of students
- Grounded in students' lives—the questions students ask become the starting point for curriculum; curriculum is generative
- Offers a safe place—all voices and interpretations must be honored, with the idea that opinions and positions can be interrogated
- Takes a critical stance—curriculum involves studying the systems of meaning and of culture; the questions asked lead to new questions
- Pro-justice—deliberate action is taken toward justice and equity
- Activist—critical curriculum informs and encourages students toward social action

---

Reflection Point 7.3 _____

1. What insights into teaching and learning have you gained from taking this journey into these two classrooms?

2. How will you be more responsive to the multiple voices and diverse needs of your students?

3. Share your ideas with colleagues at your school or in other professional groups and organizations, and seek to find collaborative partners as you work toward keeping kids in sight.

Conclusion

Throughout this book, we have shared our reflections, stories, and growing understandings of stance, social positioning, and interpretive authority. The relationships forged among these influences brought to our attention the tensions and challenges teachers and students face as they construct, negotiate, and share interpretations and understandings. The strategies and new directions we envision for literacy instruction—particularly with technology and critical literacy—encourage us to be insightful and responsive to our students. Keeping children in sight as we plan and orchestrate effective, meaningful literacy events is the theme of the Kids InSight series. Hopefully, we have offered some new ideas to consider as you plan your literacy curriculum, and hopefully we have provided you with a map with which to discover the buried treasures in your classroom.

To conclude, we would like to leave you with a sentiment shared by Jane as she reflected on reading *Island of the Blue Dolphins*: "It's a really meaningful book. And I'd like to think they [the students] have a sense of accomplishment." With the reflections and insights gained while reading this book, we hope you, too, accomplish all that you imagine with the students you teach. Remember to celebrate these accomplishments and the discovery of these hidden influences as you share your treasures with others.

Classroom Data Analysis

The data used to illustrate our findings were gathered over a 5-month period in the two classrooms and involved a variety of literacy events. To help us understand the instructional practices of the teachers and the ways in which students responded, we collected numerous data samples, including field notes, transcripts of literature discussions, transcripts of partner events, transcripts of teacher and student interviews, artifacts of students' work, and video- and audiotapes of interviews and researcher-designed activities. The data were then analyzed using a primarily qualitative research methodology. Observing the classroom context where students and teachers interact with each other and texts enabled us to gain insights into the complexities of the meaning-making process and to better understand the significant roles played by the hidden influences of stance, social positioning, and interpretive authority in literacy events. In the following sections we describe the data collection phases and the ways in which the data were coded for each study.

Lynn's Third-Grade Classroom

The data collection period (September through January) was divided into five phases, some of which occurred concurrently. In Phase One, Mary conducted general observations of the classroom to observe how the teacher, Lynn, organized the day and how she integrated reading and writing activities into all subject areas. Mary witnessed this through classroom observations and informal conversations with the classroom teacher.

In Phase Two, Mary's observations and field notes focused on the situational contexts within the classroom that promoted reader intention and motivation. Additionally, Mary specifically observed the literacy events that developed the students' intention and motivation to read text and construct meaning. These observations also focused on the interactions and dialogues between students during literacy events as well as the interaction between students and Lynn. After observing the entire class, eight focal students were selected for further study. During this 2-week period, Mary also chose specific classroom literacy events on which to focus and allowed for the opportunity of the inclusion of data from other observed events in the classroom.

During Phase Three, Mary shifted from the stance of observer to that of participant-observer. Observational field notes and audiotapes concentrated on the literacy events in which the focal students participated. The events observed were both formal and informal and the situational circumstances surrounding the events were varied. As an observer, Mary sat behind or to the side of the students during large- and small-group activities and while they were "partner reading" (two children collaboratively reading a book), which limited her interaction with the students and the teacher to avoid interference. Occasionally she would partner read with students, help with spelling words, and engage in conversations. Mary also observed them on the playground and during computer class. She focused on the interactions and dialogue between the focal students and their classmates. While observing the focal students, Mary also noted what the other students did and how they participated in the various literacy events. How the individuals performed tasks and carried on conversations during the events further illuminated the types of peer interactions that promoted intention, meaning negotiation, and meaning construction.

As a participant-observer, Mary gained access into the students' unoffical and social worlds by listening to the informal conversations that occurred while they were working in small groups, partner reading, or writing stories. These glimpses of conversations offered insights into the children's intentions and motivations for reading and writing, and they provided many opportunities to listen to students negotiate and construct meanings of text. Such opportunities also revealed clues about students' social positions and networks in the classroom, how they perceived themselves in relation to others in their class, and how they perceived others as viable partners to work with.

During Phase Four, Mary implemented two researcher-designed procedures: structured interviews and the Photo-Sorting Activity. She conducted structured interviews using the Reader/Writer Inventory (see Figure 9, page 85) with the focal students beginning in the seventh week of the study. Each interview lasted between 30 and 40 minutes. The Photo-Sorting Activity lasted 30 minutes and was administered following the ninth week.

In Phase Five, Mary inductively analyzed the data, together with the observational segment (Phase Three) and the interview/activity segment (Phase Four). Analysis of all collected data sources continued for an extensive period following the 5 months spent at the research site. Informal interviews with the teacher throughout the course of the study also provided data about reader intention, motivation, and negotiation, as well as the goals of the teacher, which emphasized the construction of meaning. (See Table 1 on page 146 for an event analysis.)

Jane and Kathy's Fourth-Grade Classroom

The data collection period (September through February) was divided into four phases. Phase One was the preliminary phase, whereby Amy observed the classroom practices and activities on an informal basis for a couple of weeks. She talked with the teachers about their instructional approaches to curriculum, the literature selections they were to use, and their overall planning scheme. During this time, the students became accustomed to the routines and structures of this classroom.

Phase Two focused primarily on the language arts block of time. At this point, Amy adopted an observer-participant role and documented the focal students' and teachers' interactions and discussions as they participated in a variety of literacy events (such as literature discussions, skill activity work, partner reading, vocabulary development, and writing book reports). In the observer-participant role, Amy sat on the periphery of the literature discussions and partner events to hear students' "side comments" as they worked. These comments provided insight into students' perceptions of stance and social positioning.

Table 1
Event Analysis for Lynn's Classroom

Nature of Interaction

Description
- purpose
- materials

Level of Participation
- individual
- partners
- small groups
- whole class

Type of Student Choice
- student choice of partners
- student choice to volunteer
- student choice of topics
- no choice

Peer Influences
- assisting
- collaborating
- encouraging
- recommending
- competing
- distracting

Intent of Dialogic Discourse
- construct meaning
- share personal experiences
- access background knowledge
- negotiate word definitions
- extraneous

Students' Perceptions

Evaluative Criteria
- smart
- cool
- annoying
- boring
- talkative
- bossy
- helpful

Access Into Events
- choose a partner
- chosen as a partner
- volunteer
- initiate discussion

Sources of Meaning Authority
- reader/writer
- teacher
- text
- peers

Phase Three of the study occurred concurrently with Phase Two. In this phase, the focal students participated in book talks with self-selected books during the Sustained Silent Reading (SSR) time. As in Phase Two, Amy gained access into the discussions by assuming an observer-participant role. The final phase, Phase Four, consisted of conducting formal interviews with the focal students and the teachers. These interviews were held in the third and fifth months of the study.

Table 2
Event Analysis for Jane and Kathy's Classroom

Components of Literacy Event	Utterance (talk occurring in literacy event)	Participation
Literature Selection • Island of the Blue Dolphins • Otherwise Known as Sheila, the Great • The Mouse and the Motorcycle • Goosebumps • Hundred Penny Box	*Structural Form of the Utterance* • question • request • statement	*Participants* • teacher present or not • number of participants
Purpose or Focus of the Event • summarize • interpret • respond to literal-level questions • make personal connections	*Intent of the Utterance* • factual • inference • inform • invite • predict • retell • evaluate • speculate	*Type of Participation* • initiator • director • respondant
Structure of Event • individual • partner • small group • large group	*Location of Intertextual Link* • personal knowledge • personal experience • imagination • world knowledge	*Source of Engagement* • response required by teacher • response required by peer • response self-initiated

The data sources collected in the four phases were then coded and categorized to better understand the happenings in the literacy events. For purposes of this study, literacy events encompassed dialogues and tasks associated with a particular literature selection. Each event was labeled and charted according to the literature selection, the types of utterances (or talk) that occurred in the event, and the participation structures. Table 2 details the event analysis.

References

Almasi, J. (1996). A new view of discussion. In L.B. Gambrell & J.F. Almasi (Eds.), *Lively discussions! Fostering engaged reading* (pp. 2–24). Newark, DE: International Reading Association.

Archambault, R.D. (1966). *Dewey on education: Appraisals*. New York: Random House.

Bakhtin, M. (1986). *Speech genres and other late essays* (V.W. McGee, Trans., C. Emerson & M. Holquist, Eds.). Austin, TX: University of Texas Press.

Barr, R., & Dreban, R. (1991). Grouping students for reading instruction. In R. Barr, M.L. Kamil, & T. Shanahan (Eds.), *Multidisciplinary perspectives on literacy research* (pp. 91–110). Urbana, IL: National Council of Teachers of English.

Beach, R., & Anson, C. (1992). Stance and intertextuality in written discourse. *Linguistics and Education, 4*, 335–357.

Berndt, T.J. (1983a). Correlates and causes of sociometric status in childhood: A commentary on six current studies of popular, rejected, and neglected children. *Merrill-Palmer Quarterly, 29*, 439–448.

Berndt, T.J. (1983b). Social cognition, social behavior, and children's friendships. In E.T. Higgins, D. Ruble, & W. Hartup (Eds.) *Social cognition and social development* (pp. 158–189). New York: Cambridge University Press.

Bloome, D., & Bailey, F. (1992). Studying language and literacy through events, particularities, and intertextuality. In R. Beach, M. Kamil, & T. Shannahan (Eds.), *Multidisciplinary perspectives on literacy research* (pp. 181–210). Urbana, IL: National Council of Teachers of English.

Bruner, J. (1966). *Toward a theory of instruction*. Cambridge, MA: Harvard University Press.

Bruner, J. (1978). The role of dialogue in language acquisition. In A. Sinclair, R.J. Jarvelle, & W.J.M. Leveet (Eds.), *The child's conception of language*. New York: Springer.

Bruner, J. (1986). *Actual minds, possible worlds*. Cambridge, MA: Harvard University Press.

Bruner, J. (1990). *Acts of meaning*. Cambridge, MA: Harvard University Press.

Cairney, T.H. (1995). *Pathways to literacy*. London: Cassell.

Calkins, L.M. (2001). *The art of teaching reading*. New York: Longman.

Cazden, C. (1986). *Classroom discourse*. Portsmouth, NH: Heinemann.

Cazden, C. (2000, March 29). *Changing conceptions of classroom discourse.* Lecture presented at Beatrice S. & David I. Miller Education Seminar series, Indiana University, Bloomington, IN.

Davidson, J.L. (1982). The group mapping activity for instruction in reading and thinking. *Journal of Reading* (pp. 26, 52–56).

Davies, B. (1994). *Poststructuralist theory and classroom practice.* Victoria, Australia: Deakin University Press.

Dewey, J. (1897). *My pedagogic creed.* New York: E.L. Kellogg & Company.

Dewey, J. (1938). *Experience and education.* New York: Macmillan.

Dillon, D. (2000). *Kids insight: Reconsidering how to meet the literacy needs of all students.* Newark, DE: International Reading Association.

Dyson, A.H. (1989). *Multiple worlds of child writers: Friends learning to write.* New York: Teachers College Press.

Dyson, A.H. (1990) Weaving possibilities: Rethinking metaphors for early literacy development. *The Reading Teacher, 44,* 202–213.

Dyson, A.H. (1993). *Social worlds of children learning to write.* New York: Teachers College Press.

Edelsky, C. (1999). On critical whole language practice: What, why and a bit of how. In C. Edelsky (Ed.), *Making justice our project: Teachers working toward critical whole language.* Urbana, IL: National Council of Teachers of English.

Fish, S. (1980). *Is there a text in this class? The authority of interpretive communities.* Cambridge, MA: Harvard University Press.

Flint, A.S. (1997). *Building sand castles and why Ralph and Keith are friends: The influence of stance, intertextuality, and interpretive authority on meaning construction.* Unpublished doctoral dissertation, University of California, Berkeley.

Flint, A.S. (2000a). Know-it-alls, Identifiers, Defenders, and Solidifiers (KIDS): Examining interpretive authority in literacy events. *Reading Research and Instruction, 39,* 119–134.

Flint, A.S. (2000b). Reflection. *Primary voices, 9,* 30–33.

Flint, A.S., Lysaker, J., Riordan-Karlsson, M., & Molinelli, P. (1999). Converging and intersecting views: An investigation of stance in four independent classroom studies. In T. Shanahan & F. Rodriguez-Brown (Eds.), *48th yearbook of the National Reading Conference* (pp. 240–353). Chicago: National Reading Conference.

Fransella, F., & Bannister, D. (1977). *A manual or repertory grid technique.* London: Academic Press.

Garnica, O. (1981). Social dominance and classroom interaction: The omega child in the classroom. In J. Green & C. Wallat (Eds.), *Ethnography and language in educational settings* (pp. 229–252). Norwood, NJ: Ablex.

Gee, J. (1990). *Social linguistics and literacies: Ideology in discourses.* London: Falmer Press.

Harris, P.J. (1979). *Teacher's perceptions of children's reading ability and their implications on children's perceptions of reading.* Unpublished honors thesis, The University of Sydney, Sydney, Australia.

Harris, P.J. (1989). *First grade children's constructs of teacher-assigned reading tasks in a whole language classroom.* Unpublished doctoral dissertation. University of California, Berkeley, CA.

Harste, J.C., Breau, A., Leland, C., Lewison, M., Ociepka, A., & Vasquez, V. (1999). Exploring critical literacy: You can hear a pin drop. *Language Arts, 77,* 70–77.

Harste, J.C., Breau, A., Leland, C., Lewison, M., Ociepka, A., & Vasquez, V. (2000). Supporting critical conversations. In K.M. Pierce (Ed.), *Adventuring with books* (4th ed., pp. 507–554). Urbana, IL: National Council of Teachers of English.

Hartman, D.K. (1991). The intertextual links of readers using multiple passages: A postmodern/semiotic/cognitive view of meaning making. In R.B. Ruddell, M.R. Ruddell, & H. Singer (Eds.), *Theoretical models and processes of reading* (4th ed., pp. 616–636). Newark, DE: International Reading Association.

Jonassen, D.H. (1999). *Computers as mindtools for schools: Engaging critical thinking* (2nd ed.). Englewood Cliffs, NJ: Merrill.

Kamberlis, G. & Scott, K.D. (1992), Other people's voices: The coarticulation of texts and subjectivities. *Linguistics and Education, 4,* 359–403.

Langer, J. (1995). *Envisioning literature: Literary understandings and literature instruction.* New York: Teacher's College Press.

Lewis, C. (2000). Limits and identification: The personal, pleasurable, and critical in reader response. *Journal of Literacy Research, 32,* 253–266.

Lewison, M., & Heffernan, L. (2000). *Critical conversations and social issues in the elementary school* (Videotape). Bloomington, IN: Language Education Department, Indiana University.

Luke, A., & Freebody, P. (1997). The social practices of reading. In S. Muspratt, A. Luke, & P. Freebody (Eds.), *Constructing critical literacies* (pp. 185–225). Cresskill, NJ: Hampton Press.

McGinley, W., Kamberelis, G., Mahoney, T., Madigan, D., Rybicki, V., & Oliver, J. (1997). Re-visioning reading and teaching literature through the lens of narrative theory. In T. Rogers & A.O. Soter (Eds.), *Reading across cultures: Teaching literature in a diverse society* (pp. 42–68). New York: Teachers College Press.

McMahon, S., & Raphael, T. (1997). The book club program: Theoretical and research foundations. In S. McMahon, T. Raphael, V. Goatley, & L. Pardo (Eds.), *The book club connection: Literacy learning and classroom talk* (pp. 3–25). New York: Teachers College Press; Newark, DE: International Reading Association.

McMahon, S., Raphael, T., Goatley, V., & Pardo, L. (Eds.). (1997). *The book club connection: Literacy learning and classroom talk.* New York: Teachers College Press; Newark, DE: International Reading Association.

Mehan, H. (1979). *Learning lessons.* Cambridge, MA: Harvard University Press.

Ogle, D. (1986). K-W-L: A teaching model that develops active reading of expository text. *The Reading Teacher, 39,* 564–570.

Palinscar, A., & Brown, A. (1984.) Reciprocal teaching of comprehension-fostering and comprehension-monitoring activities. *Cognition and Instruction, 1,* 117–175.

Pappas, C., Kiefer, B., & Levstik, L. (1999). *An integrated language perspective in the elementary school: An action approach* (3rd ed.). Reading, MA: Addison-Wesley.

Paterson, B. (1994). Teaching for social justice: One teacher's journey. In B. Bigelow (Ed.), *Rethinking our classrooms: Teaching for equity and justice* (pp. 40–41). Milwaukee, WI: Rethinking Schools.

Probst, R. (1990). *Five kinds of literary knowing* (Report Series 5.5). Albany, NY: Center for the Learning and Teaching of Literature.

Raphael, T. (1982). Questions-answering strategies for children. *The Reading Teacher, 36,* 186–190.

Raphael, T. (1986). Teaching question-answer relationship, revisited. *The Reading Teacher, 39,* 516–523.

Riordan-Karlsson, M. (1997). *Negotiations, friendships, and chapter books: The influence of meaning authority, peer interaction, and student perceptions on reader motivation and meaning construction in a third grade classroom.* Unpublished doctoral dissertation, University of California, Berkeley, CA.

Riordan-Karlsson, M. (1999). *Constructivism.* Westminister, CA: Teacher Created Materials.

Rogoff, B. (1990). *Apprenticeship in thinking.* New York: Oxford University Press.

Rosenblatt, L.M. (1978). *The reader, the text, the poem: The transactional theory of the literary work.* Carbondale, IL: Southern Illinois University Press.

Rosenblatt, L.M. (1983). *Literature as exploration* (4th ed.). New York: Modern Language Association. (Original work published 1938)

Rosenblatt, L.M. (1994). The transactional theory of reading and writing. In R.B. Ruddell, M.R. Ruddell, & H. Singer (Eds.), *Theoretical models and processes of reading* (4th ed., pp. 1057–1092). Newark, DE: International Reading Association.

Ruddell, R.B., & Ruddell, M.R. (1994). *Teaching children to read and write: Becoming an influential teacher.* Boston: Allyn & Bacon.

Ruddell, R.B., & Unrau, N. (1994). Reading as a meaning construction process: The reader, the text, and the teacher. In R.B. Ruddell, M.R. Ruddell, & H. Singer (Eds.), *Theoretical models and processes of reading* (4th ed., pp. 996–1056). Newark, DE: International Reading Association.

Scherer, P. (1996). Book club through a fishbowl: Extensions to early elementary classrooms. In S. McMahon, T. Raphael, V. Goatley, & L. Pardo (Eds.), *The book club connection: Literacy learning and classroom talk* (pp. 250–263). New York: Teachers College Press; Newark, DE: International Reading Association.

Short, K., & Harste, J., with Burke, C. (1996). *Creating classrooms for authors and inquirers.* Portsmouth, NH: Heinemann.

Stauffer, R.G. (1976). *Teaching reading as a thinking process.* New York: Harper & Row.

Vogt, M. (1996). Creating a response-centered curriculum with literature discussion groups. In L.B. Gambrell & J.F. Almasi (Eds.), *Lively discussions! Fostering engaged reading* (pp. 181–193). Newark, DE: International Reading Association.

Vygotsky, L. (1978). *Mind in society: The development of higher psychological processes* (M. Cole, V. John-Steiner, S. Scribner, & E. Souberman, Eds. and Trans.). Cambridge, MA: Harvard University Press. (Original work published 1934)

Wertsch, J.V. (1991). *Voices of the mind: A sociocultural approach to mediated action.* Cambridge, MA: Harvard University Press.

West, J. (1996). Getting help when you need it: The relations between social status and third graders' helping interactions during literacy events. In D.J. Leu, C.K. Kinzer, & K.A. Hinchman (Eds.), *45th yearbook of the National Reading Conference*. Chicago, IL: National Reading Conference.

Wiencek, J., & O'Flahavan, J. (1994). From teacher-led to peer discussions about literature: Suggestions for making the shift. *Language Arts, 71*, 488–498.

Wigfield, A. (1995). Children's motivations for reading and reading engagement. In J.T. Guthrie & A. Wigfield (Eds.), *Reading engagement: Motivating reading through integrated instruction* (pp. 14–33). Newark, DE: International Reading Association.

Wood, D., Bruner, J.S., & Ross, B. (1976). The role of tutoring in problem solving. *Journal of Child Psychology and Psychiatry, 17*, 89–100.

Children's Book References

Blume, J. (1972). *Otherwise known as Sheila, the great*. New York: Dell.

Brown, J. (1996). *Flat Stanley*. New York: Harper Trophy.

Cameron, A. (1989). *More stories Julian tells*. New York: Random House.

Cherry, L. (1990). *The great kapok tree: A tale of the amazon rain forest*. New York: Voyager Picture Books.

Cleary, B. (1965). *The mouse and the motorcycle*. New York: Avon.

Dagliesh, A. (1991). *The courage of Sarah Noble*. New York: Aladdin.

Golenbach, P. (1990). *Teammates*. New York: Harcourt.

Hesse, K. (1998). *just [sic] Juice*. New York: Scholastic.

Keene, C. (1930). *Nancy Drew*. New York: Simon & Schuster.

MacLachlan, P. (1987). *Sarah, plain and tall*. New York: Harper Trophy.

Mathis, S. (1975). *Hundred penny box*. New York: Scholastic.

O'Dell, S. (1960). *Island of the blue dolphins*. New York: Dell.

Perrault, C. (1983). *Puss in boots*. Ill. Paul Galdone. Boston: Houghton Mifflin.

Schur, M.R. (1986). *Samantha's surprise: A Christmas story*. Middleton, WI: Pleasant Company Publications.

Seldon, G. (1989). *The cricket in Times Square*. New York: Dell.

Shaw, B. (1986). *Meet Kristen: An American girl*. Middleton, WI: Pleasant Company Publications.

Stine, R.L. (1995). *Goosebumps: Night of terror tower*. New York: Scholastic.

Stine, R.L. (1995). *Goosebumps: The night of the living dummy*. New York: Scholastic.

Tripp, V. (1986). *Meet Molly: An American girl*. Middleton, WI: Pleasant Company Publications.

Tripp, V. (1991). *Meet Felicity: An American girl*. Middleton, WI: Pleasant Company Publications.

White, E.B. (1974). *Stuart Little*. New York: Harper Trophy.

Index

Page references followed by *b, f,* or *t* indicate boxes, figures, or tables, respectively.